# How to Start and Run Your Own Home-based Business

**Matthew Thomas**

publishing

First published in 2009 by
**W & H Publishing**
Apple Tree Cottage, Inlands Road, Nutbourne, PO18 8RJ

**Text and Cover Design** Wendy Craig
**Printed and Bound** in the UK by CPI Antony Rowe

**British Library Cataloguing in Publication Data**
A CIP record for this book is available from the British Library
ISBN 978-0-9561091-0-1

## Introduction

'May you live in interesting times' is, so I am told, an old Chinese curse. The implication is that most of us would far rather live in ordinary, even slightly dull, times. Interesting times suggests times of insecurity, of disruption, of change. And most of us, while we may agree that 'a change is as good as a rest', are uneasy when the world appears to be changing almost daily before our eyes.

Well, like it or not, few would deny that these are interesting times. Seldom has the pace of change in the world been more rapid. And nowhere has this been felt more than in the world of work. In the UK at least, the last ten years have seen the virtual collapse of manufacturing industry. The whole concept of 'a job for life' has vanished, with many people facing redundancy not just once, but two, three times or more during their careers. Even in sectors that were previously bywords for stability, such as banking and insurance, large-scale redundancies have become the norm. Many jobs advertised today are not permanent – whatever permanent might mean now – but on short-term contracts. And the global financial downturn of 2008 has further destabilised the employment market. As a result of all these factors, very few people today have the luxury of knowing that they will still have a job this time next year.

All change, however, brings opportunities as well as threats – and I firmly believe that as a result of some of these social and economic changes the prospects for people wanting to start a business of their own have never been better. Many of the organisations that laid off staff now buy in services from freelances or small businesses. Advice and assistance is widely – and in many cases freely – available for people who want to start up on their own. And advances in information and communications technology (computers, mobile phones, the Internet and so on) mean that self-employed people and small businesses can compete more effectively than ever before with large corporations. These developments have also, of course, created a wealth of (home-based) business opportunities for people with relevant skills, such as website designers, computer programmers, and so on.

Starting your own business is far more than just a substitute for traditional employment, however – it is a positive career choice in its own right. With many jobs today offering little in the way of satisfaction or prospects, more people than ever are looking for alternative ways of finding fulfilment in their work. Not only that, many are seeking more flexible working arrangements that allow them to enjoy more time with their families or pursuing leisure interests. Running your own home-based business – in which I also include businesses such as gardening and window cleaning where you work mainly on customers' premises – can provide great satisfaction and the potential of good financial rewards, and it can be as flexible as you wish. A home-based business is also, of course, ideal for many people with disabilities. As a result of all these factors, starting a home-based business has become for many people their favoured route to achieving the life they desire for themselves and their loved ones. Every year, thousands more people are 'breaking free' to enjoy the flexibility of self-employment and the satisfactions and rewards of being their own boss. This book will show you how you can join them...

So why did I write How to Start and Run Your Own Home-Based Business? For nearly twenty years I have run a successful home-based writing and consultancy business, specialising in careers and self-development. During this time I have met many other home-based workers in a wide range of occupations. Without exception, they all agreed that starting in business was one of the best decisions they ever made, and not one (except on a very bad day) ever expressed any wish to be back in a conventional job. I believe that, for many people, starting a home-based business can be the answer to unemployment, job insecurity, work-based stress and the lack of flexibility in traditional employment. If this book serves to ease the path of just one person into the exciting world of running their own business, I shall be more than satisfied.

I'd like to close with a word of thanks and an appeal. Thanks must go first to the many home-based workers and organisations assisting them who helped me in researching and writing this book. And the appeal? I should like to ask you, valued reader, to write to me via my publishers if you have found this book helpful, or you have any suggestions for the next edition. And if, as a result of reading this book, you set up a home-based business of your own, I should be delighted to hear about it.

I wish you every success.

# chapter 1

## Why start your own business?

In the UK, and many other countries as well, starting your own business has never been more popular. According to a report from the GEM Project (Global Entrepreneurship Monitor), in 2006 over 2.7 million people in the UK were attempting to start a business of their own. Less encouragingly, around 500,000 UK businesses close down every year (source: Barclays Bank). So why, despite the obvious risks, are so many people drawn to starting businesses of their own? Their reasons are as varied as the individuals themselves, but the most common include the following.

### 1. To Make More Money

It's a well-known saying, but nonetheless true: nobody ever got rich working for someone else. If you run your own business, the profits will go into your pockets rather than those of someone else (who probably has more than enough already...). If your business does well, you can make a lot of money – certainly more than you could ever earn doing a similar job for someone else.

### 2. To Be Independent

In our fast-changing world, few if any jobs now offer long-term security, let alone opportunities for career progression. For many people, one major attraction of starting their own business is to obtain the security now seldom available in paid employment. By starting a successful business they hope to obtain greater independence and financial security for themselves and their loved ones, and perhaps in the long term generate a valuable legacy to pass on to their children.

### 3. To Gain Personal Satisfaction and Fulfilment

This is a very important reason, especially for people whose current circumstances give them little of either. Being your own boss gives you a measure of freedom and power. You have the chance to exercise and develop your existing skills and learn new ones, and every day to face the excitement of fresh challenges.

### 4. To Obtain Higher Status in the Eyes of Others

Though some may be jealous of their achievements, in general successful business people are held in high esteem by others in the community. By providing goods or services, perhaps employing other people, and paying taxes and duties, they make a real contribution to their community and the quality of life of everyone in it.

### 5. To Follow Through an Idea or Invention

This is not the most common reason, but many businesses exist because the owner had an idea or spotted a gap in the market, and saw an opportunity to make money from it.

Many people think from time to time about starting a business, but frequently it goes no further than that. Often it takes the spur of a sudden change in circumstances for vague plans to crystallise into something more definite. So perhaps one more reason should be added to this list:

## 6. To Escape from a Sudden, Unwelcome Change in Circumstances

The most common example is unemployment caused by redundancy, but there may also be changes that make your position at work uncomfortable or even untenable. For example, a reorganisation may mean that the nature of your job changes fundamentally, or a new manager may be appointed who decides your face no longer fits in his (or her) department. Or the change may be nothing to do with your job: perhaps for family reasons it becomes essential for you to spend more time at home (e.g. to care for an elderly relative). Any of these circumstances may provide the incentive for people to seriously consider setting up on their own.

All these reasons and more are potential advantages of starting your own business. There are, however, some possible drawbacks as well, and this is something to be aware of when deciding whether starting a business would be right for you.

## 1. Possible Variations of Income

Instead of having a 'secure' regular weekly or monthly income, a business owner depends for his income on the success of the business, and this is likely to vary from month to month. Of course, an employee's sense of security may well be illusory; if the company employing him is unsuccessful, he will soon find himself out of a job. However, a large business is often able to absorb a temporary downturn in its fortunes by cutting costs and drawing on reserves, so employees are less quickly and directly affected by their employer's difficulties. A business owner, on the other hand, suffers an immediate loss of income if his business passes through a difficult period.

## 2. Sacrifices

Starting a new enterprise may involve sacrifices both for you and your family. Many businessmen and women have sacrificed their career prospects in a large organisation in order to go out on their own. If you decide to be your own boss and it doesn't work out, you may find it difficult to re-enter paid employment for someone else. During the business's first few years it may be hard to find time for a holiday or leisure activities. There may also be financial sacrifices, as in the early years most of the profits from the business may have to be re-invested or used to pay off loans. In the short term, you and your family's general standard of living may well be reduced.

## 3. Hard Work and Stress

In spite of the apparent freedom of being your own boss, the early years of a new business generally require you to work longer hours than you did before. You will have to bear all the stress and worry of the business, and will probably carry this with you even when you are not actually working. There can also be a sense of loneliness and isolation. Many people who decide to set up in business begin (at least) on their own. One common complaint among such people is that they miss the day-to-day banter of the office or shop floor. They also miss having colleagues to turn to when it comes to making difficult decisions or solving problems.

Although at first sight the above may appear rather daunting, it is important not to over-emphasise the possible drawbacks. The truth is that for many people, especially those of a go-getting and entrepreneurial temperament, the attractions and advantages of starting a business greatly outweigh them. One message that should come through clearly, however, is that running your own business is far more than just a means of making a living: it is, quite literally, a way of life. It therefore requires commitment and self-belief, both on your part and that of your family. This is discussed in more detail in the next chapter.

# chapter 2

## Requirements for success

Deciding to start your own business is unlike applying for a job in one very important respect. While selection for a job usually depends on filling in an application form and attending for interview, no-one else chooses you for self-employment – you must decide for yourself whether you are suitable. Just as it is important to look at your reasons for starting a business, therefore, it is important to examine the qualities and skills you possess personally. These are not simply the specific product- or service-related skills needed for the business you intend to start (essential though these of course are). Rather, they are the general skills and qualities everyone starting in business must have.

So what are the personal qualities you need to succeed in business? Here are the answers some businessmen and women gave themselves.

> *By far the biggest quality is determination. If things don't go right at first, you have to keep on. Everyone's allowed to make a few mistakes. The main thing is not to be put off when you hit snags.*

Eric Lunn, Director, Hinges & Things

> *Always remember that failure is merely a stepping stone to success. When things go wrong (and they will!), pick yourself up, dust yourself down, and start again. You've learned what doesn't work. Now try it a different way. Don't resist failure: it's essential to being brilliant in business. He who never fails, never wins!*

Karl Moore, Managing Director, White Cliff Computing Ltd
www.karlmoore.com

> *You have to commit yourself to it. If you see an opportunity, however small, you must pursue it relentlessly. If you go into business half-heartedly or with your fingers crossed behind your back, then you're likely to fail.*

Mr F.M. Dawson, Proprietor, Framada Materials Handling

> *You have to be dedicated, maybe even a bit obsessed! Bags of energy and enthusiasm to get you through the difficult times, which there will be. And, in my line anyway, if helps if you like people and get on with them.*

Frances Look, freelance photographer

> *You need determination, to work long hours – especially at the start, and never give up. Don't let disappointments deter you or affect your morale. But the rewards make all the effort worth it.*

Anthony Todd, Managing Director, East Cheshire Printers

> *A need to provide a high level of service and to understand customer requirements and explore ways of serving their needs in a most cost effective manner.*

Mary Lees, Director, Sawyers Packaging

As these quotes reveal, everyone has different views on which qualities are the most important for success in business, but there are certain requirements that come up time and time again.

*(1) Determination*

Many people talk about starting a business, but only a small proportion do anything about it. Starting a business is a major decision that will change your life and that of your family. It is important that you are committed to your new career before making such a move; and that once you have started the business you are determined to see it through to success.

*(2) Willingness to Work*

We all think we are willing to work hard, but if you start a business you will soon find out what this means in practice! In the early days at least you are likely to have to work longer hours than the average employee. Although as your business becomes established some of the pressure may ease, you must still expect to work longer and harder than most people in paid employment.

*(3) Persistence and Perseverance*

Successful business people let nothing get in the way of achieving their goals. If they encounter problems, they try to find ways to overcome them. If their first attempt does not succeed, they try a different approach; and, if this doesn't work, another. They are not put off by pitfalls, or discouraged – other than temporarily – by failure. They persevere in their efforts until, eventually, they do succeed.

*(4) Stamina*

In view of the hours you are likely to have to put in, stamina and at least reasonably good health are important. People running businesses have to avoid taking time off for sickness if at all possible. As a self-employed sole trader in particular, if you are not working you are not generating any income. And if you let down a customer, next time he is likely to go elsewhere.

*(5) Self-discipline*

If you are in a paid job the chances are you will have a manager or supervisor, part of whose duty is to ensure that you fulfil your obligations to your employer. Your reasons for wishing to start a business may include escaping from such individuals! However, while as a business owner you will have no-one standing watch over you, you will still have obligations to customers, suppliers, employees, officials, and so on. If your business is to go on running successfully, it is important that you have the self-discipline to fulfil all your responsibilities and see a job through to the end.

*(6) Willingness to Take Risks*

All business people have to take calculated risks. Whereas in a job you have the relative security of a regular wage or salary, as a self-employed person there is no guarantee what your income will be from one month to the next. You will constantly find yourself having to make decisions about where and how to advertise, which areas to specialise in, when to invest in new equipment, and so on. Although this constant decision-making can be stressful, it can also be satisfying and enjoyable. Solving problems and making decisions can give you a sense of power and confidence.

*(7) Ability to Cope with Stress*

Starting and running a business inevitably imposes a range of stresses, both on the businessman himself and on his family. In the beginning at least, long hours, hard work and disruption to family life can cause tension. To be successful in business you need to be able to cope with, and even thrive on, this kind of pressure.

*(8) Enthusiasm*

Enthusiasm is an essential ingredient of every businessman. If you are half-hearted about your new venture you may have difficulty summoning sufficient determination to overcome problems when they arise. If you are enthusiastic, on the other hand, you will relish the challenges your business presents. What's more, your enthusiasm will rub off onto customers, employees (if you have them) and other people you have to deal with. Most of us would far rather work with or buy from someone who is enthusiastic and enjoys his work, rather than someone who is permanently depressed about it.

## (9) Ambition

Most business people have a driving ambition to achieve the best they can for themselves and their loved ones: as well as money, this may include financial security and a better way of life. With such ambitions they can cope with any setbacks along the way, because in their mind they have a goal or vision that drives them on. Ambition and determination together can overcome many obstacles. In business, as in most others aspects of life, if you know what you want and are determined to achieve it, the chances are excellent that you will succeed.

## (10) Honesty and Willingness to Give Good Service

Every business depends for its continuing survival on a circle of satisfied customers. If people are pleased with the service they have received from you, they are likely to recommend you to others as well as keep coming back themselves. By contrast, if you give poor service then, even if they do not complain at the time, they will not return; and rather than recommend you to others, they will warn them about you. If you have a good reputation this will ensure that more people keep coming to you. For this reason, successful business people go to great lengths to obtain and keep a good name for themselves.

## EXERCISE

To help assess whether you have the necessary personal qualities for starting and running your own business, complete the checklist below. Circle or underline the description which best describes you.

| | | 1 | 2 | 3 | 4 |
|---|---|---|---|---|---|
| 1. | I enjoy a challenge | always | usually | sometimes | never |
| 2. | I am willing to work long hours | always | usually | sometimes | never |
| 3. | I actively seek out new experiences | always | usually | sometimes | never |
| 4. | I am good at taking responsibility | always | usually | sometimes | never |
| 5. | I am willing to take criticism | always | usually | sometimes | never |
| 6. | I am good at organising my own time | always | usually | sometimes | never |
| 7. | I am self-confident | always | usually | sometimes | never |
| 8. | My general health is good | always | usually | sometimes | never |
| 9. | I am known as honest and reliable | certainly | probably | possibly | unlikely |
| 10. | I expect a lot of myself and the people I work with | always | usually | sometimes | never |
| 11. | I believe success depends on | myself | myself and others | a range of factors | luck |
| 12. | I view failure as | an opportunity to learn | an annoyance | a disappointment | a disaster |
| 13. | In a group situation people look to me to provide leadership | always | usually | sometimes | never |
| 14. | I can recognise when I need help | always | usually | sometimes | never |
| 15. | I look for feedback on my performance so that I can do better next time | always | usually | sometimes | never |
| 16. | I am a good judge of character | always | usually | sometimes | never |
| 17. | I can delegate to others when appropriate | always | usually | sometimes | never |
| 18. | I can cope with uncertainty about my job and my income | very easily | fairly easily | with some difficulty | with great difficulty |
| 19. | I carry on until a job is complete | always | usually | sometimes | never |
| 20. | I can cope with stress | always | usually | sometimes | never |

Now score your responses, giving four points for an answer in column (1), three points for an answer in column (2), two points for an answer in column (3) and one point for an answer in column (4).

If your total is 70 or more, you appear to have the required personal qualities to make a success of starting and running your own business.

If you scored 60–70, you have most of the qualities, but may need to work on certain aspects of your temperament and personality.

If you scored 45–60, you should be able to make a success of starting and running a business, but some areas will definitely need attention.

If you scored 45 or less, you may need to think hard about whether you have the right personal qualities for self-employment.

This exercise should give you some idea as to how well suited you are personally to self-employment. However, people are not always as honest as they could be in assessing their strengths and weaknesses, and sometimes they have an unrealistic view of themselves. It is therefore not a bad idea to copy the above questionnaire and ask your partner, close friend or a relative who knows you well to complete it on your behalf. Compare the answers they provide for you with the answers you gave yourself. Where there are differences, or you disagree with the answer they have given, ask them (in a non-confrontational manner) why they responded that way. Explain that you are not criticising them or the way they completed the task, but simply want to understand your own strengths and weaknesses better.

On the other hand, if the total score given by your partner, friend or relative comes out significantly higher than the score you gave yourself, you may be under-estimating yourself. This may be an encouraging sign that you should have more confidence in your abilities and aptitude for starting and running a business. But do check with the person concerned that they gave honest answers and were not simply trying to please or flatter you!

## Friends and Family

Just as it is important to have the right personal qualities yourself, you will also need a supportive family and friends. If you decide to start your business from home, this will inevitably cause changes and disruption in the family routine. Even if you use separate business premises, your friends and family will still have to come to terms with your working long hours and having less time and energy for leisure activities. If you are married or living together, it is especially important that your partner understands the implications of your setting up in business, and supports what you are trying to do.

There is also a positive side, of course. Your family may be a valuable source of help in all sorts of areas, from answering the phone and writing letters, to book-keeping and assisting customers. Having others closely involved with the business can assist when problems arise, as they will bring different ideas and perspectives to the situation. Although it is not absolutely essential to have a supportive family, there is no doubt that you are much more likely to succeed if you have discussed your plans with them and have their wholehearted support.

## CHECKLIST

Complete this simple checklist, underlining the answer which applies.

| | |
|---|---|
| Have you discussed your plans for starting a business with your family? | yes / no |
| Do they, on the whole, support your plans? | yes / no |
| Are they willing to assist in the business? | yes / no |
| Do any of them have useful skills which complement your own? (e.g. book-keeping, selling, typing, foreign languages, computers, etc.) | yes / no |
| Will they be able to cope with a variable income? | yes / no |
| Have they accepted that there may be a drop in their standards of living? | yes / no |
| Does anyone else in the family have a job or other source of income which could tide you over while the business is becoming established? | yes / no |
| Could your family cope without you for housework, childcare, gardening, repairs, and so on? | yes / no |

The more of the above you can answer 'yes' to, the better your chances of success are likely to be.

## Your Skills

To run your business successfully, as well as the right personal qualities and a supportive family and friends, you will need a range of skills. These are described in general terms below. If you lack any of these it does not necessarily mean that you should not set up in business. However, if you feel any of these areas is going to present serious problems, you may need to consider taking on a partner or employee to handle that aspect of the business, or using a specialist adviser or consultant. You might also consider taking other courses to acquire the skills you need.

### (1) Technical Skills

These are the skills that you need to actually make the products or deliver the service you are offering. For some types of business you will need to have relevant experience (probably gained as an employee) and perhaps some professional qualifications. For instance, no-one today would set up as a car mechanic without at least some relevant training and experience. On the other hand, for other types of business, for example commission selling or odd-jobbing, specific qualifications and experience may not be essential. Whatever your business, however, if you expect people to pay you for your work, you will need to have the necessary technical skills to deliver a good quality product or service.

### (2) Financial

To run a business successfully you will need a range of financial skills. These include skills in such matters as book-keeping, negotiating credit terms with suppliers, invoicing, credit control, estimating, drawing up budgets and controlling cash flow (the flow of money into and out of the business).

*(3) Marketing*

Marketing is the process by which you identify potential customers and persuade them to buy your products or services. It includes selling skills, and also such matters as pricing, advertising, sales promotions, public relations, and market research.

*(4) Management*

If you are going to employ others, you will need a variety of management skills in such areas as recruitment, motivating staff and team building. You will need a knowledge of employment law and health and safety requirements. You will also need to be able to fulfil legal requirements in matters such as deducting tax from employees' pay.

*(5) Organisation*

Whether or not you intend to employ others, you will need organisational skills to ensure that every aspect of your business runs smoothly. This includes setting up systems for dealing with orders and enquiries, keeping customer records, and so on. It also includes time management, i.e. ensuring that your time is used as efficiently as possible.

*(6) Planning*

Every businessman also needs planning skills. Good financial planning is crucial to the success of a business. Planning skills are also needed to take best advantage of new opportunities that may present themselves, and to avoid any problems due to changing market conditions. Good planning can avert many problems before they happen.

Many of these skills can be acquired through taking courses, reading books (including this one!), talking to professional advisers, and so on. They will also develop naturally with practice and experience once your business is up and running. However, if you are to succeed in running a business of your own, the above are the most important skills you will need to master.

# chapter 3

## The benefits of working from home...

There are many practical advantages to running your business from home. Some of the main ones are listed in this chapter.

*Save money* – If you work from home you will avoid having to pay rent and other running costs (including business rates) on business premises. You will also save on travel expenses (see below).

*Save on travel* – You also avoid wasting many potentially productive hours in your car or on public transport. Many people (e.g. with jobs in London and other major cities) spend two or more hours a day just commuting; added up over a year, the total amount of time 'lost' in this way can be quite staggering. With many roads approaching gridlock during the morning and evening rush hours, the savings in terms of both time and your blood pressure can be substantial. You will save money on petrol and season tickets; and a further benefit is that you will avoid having to venture out every day during the winter months on dangerous, icy roads and pavements. Of course, you will still have to do some travelling, for reasons such as going to the bank or post office, visiting clients and selling your work.

*Feel more comfortable* – For a start, you can wear whatever clothes you like. You don't even have to dress or shave if you don't wish (though you will, of course, need to make an effort with your appearance when meeting clients and selling your services). You can take tea, coffee and meal breaks as you like, whenever it happens to suit you. You can also arrange your office furniture, lighting and so on exactly as you prefer.

*Benefit from flexibility* – Many aspects of family life can be easier to arrange if you work from home. For example, if you want to pop out at 3.30 to collect your youngest child from school, there is nothing (and no-one) to stop you. You can choose your own hours, working early in the morning or late at night if these options suit you best. You can be around during the day when the plumber or the meter reader calls; you can put out the washing and bring it back in if it starts to rain; and you will not miss important deliveries because you are toiling away at a separate workplace.

*Enjoy tax advantages* – If you work from home you may be able to claim a proportion of your household expenses (heating, lighting, mortgage/rent, etc.) against tax. Any alterations or repairs to the property which are directly relevant to your business activity may also be set against your business income. You should, however, note that if you make major changes to your home to accommodate your business, you may require planning permission from the council and become liable to pay business rates. You may also become liable for Capital Gains Tax if you subsequently sell your home.

*Gain greater home security* – The fact that you are likely to be around in the day can help deter burglars (most burglaries in residential areas take place during the daytime). You will also be on the premises – and therefore able to take prompt action – in the event of fires, burst pipes and other such emergencies. Some insurance companies are starting to recognise this fact and offer lower premiums for homeworkers – though this must be set against the fact that work-related computers and other equipment may have to be insured separately for an additional premium (see Chapter 21, *Insurance*).

*Enlist support from your family* – Working from home means you may be able to get help from your family in your business activities. This might include such matters as answering the phone, making appointments, typing invoices and letters, meeting and greeting visitors, and providing other forms of practical assistance (e.g. repairing the car or troubleshooting your brand new multimedia computer which obstinately refuses to function!).

*Enjoy the lack of pressure* – With a home-based business you can work as many or as few hours as you wish. If you want to work a fifteen-hour day, you can do so (though hopefully not every day!). Equally, however, you can work part-time if you prefer, perhaps to fit in with your family responsibilities. You can also set your own pace, with no-one standing over you telling you to work harder or faster. For older people, or those with disabilities that slow them down, this can be a particular attraction. As long as your business is bringing in enough money to meet your needs and those of your dependants, you can work as hard or as lightly as you wish – you have complete control over your 'terms and conditions'. It should, however, be emphasised that, although you won't have a boss looking over your shoulder, you will still have customers, who will expect a good quality product or service from you within a certain deadline.

# chapter 4

## ...and a few drawbacks

Although working from home has many attractions, it does possess a few potential drawbacks as well. Some of the main points to consider are set out in this chapter.

*May disrupt family life* – Running a business from home means you and your family's domestic lives will inevitably be affected. Obviously you will need a space in the house to work that might otherwise be used by other family members. In addition, many self-employed individuals have to work long and irregular hours, and your family may need to get used to you being in and out at all times. You may have to work during the evenings, public holidays and weekends, when most 'normal' people are at leisure. Furthermore, in many businesses clients may wish to contact you by phone outside standard office hours (this applies especially if you provide a service to private individuals, e.g. window cleaning or gardening). Family members will therefore need to become accustomed to receiving calls from clients and be briefed on how to handle them. If you have other heavy phone users in the house (e.g. teenagers!) you may need to consider having a separate line installed for business calls.

*May be too many distractions* – Family and domestic matters can also interfere with your business. Friends and relatives who would never dream of interrupting you at a 'proper' job may think nothing of phoning up or arriving unannounced, not realising (or perhaps caring) that you are 'at work'. Regular interruptions of this nature can seriously reduce your productivity, and hence your income. Even if you avoid this problem, working from home offers a huge range of potential distractions, from pets and family matters, through shopping and household chores, to gardening and watching television. You will need to be self-disciplined, or you can fritter away many working hours on non-productive (in business terms, at least) activities such as these.

*May be lonely* – Running a business from home can be lonely at times. This applies especially if you live on your own, where in some businesses (e.g. freelance writing or computer programming) you may not speak to another person face-to-face (apart from perhaps the post office clerk) for days on end. Even if you do have a family – or at least a spouse/partner – you may find the isolation during the day difficult to bear. This applies especially if you have previously worked in a busy office or factory, or you have a naturally sociable temperament.

*Clients may be deterred* – Customers who come to see you in person may be put off to find that you work from home. However unreasonably, they may deduce from this that you are not serious about your business and that you might fail to deliver a professional standard of product or service. Even if you conduct your business entirely by mail, some people find what is obviously the use of a private address off-putting. You can get around this problem to some extent by using a PO Box (see Chapter 12, *Help from the Post Office*) or a separate accommodation address.

*Can be hard to get away from work* – If you work from home, you may find that work and domestic life become indivisible and it is very hard to 'switch off' and relax when the day's work is done. People who have previously worked in a separate establishment often find the journey between home and workplace provides a valuable psychological dividing line. When your home is also your workplace this line is gone, and the distinction between work and leisure can therefore easily become blurred.

*May need greater home security* – If you have high-value, easily portable equipment such as computers, fax machines and so on, this may make your home a tempting target for burglars. If, as with many businesses, you have to publicise your address on letterheads, advertisements and so on, this will unfortunately increase the risk of your property being targeted. You may therefore need to increase the level of security in your home, perhaps fitting a burglar alarm, security lighting/cameras, window locks, and so on.

*Planning and other restrictions may apply* – There are often planning restrictions on running businesses from homes in residential areas. This is most likely to be a problem if your proposed business is likely to cause noise or other irritation to your neighbours: printing, for example, or car repairs. If you live in rented accommodation, the landlord may object to your running a business from his property; and if you are buying your house with the aid of a loan or mortgage, the lenders may be unhappy. There may also be terms in the lease or deeds of your property prohibiting its use for business purposes. And there is a possibility that running a business from home may mean that you become liable for business rates as well as your normal council tax. This and similar matters are further discussed in Chapter 7, *Planning Permission and Business Rates*.

None of these problems is insurmountable, but it is undoubtedly true that working from home is more likely to be suitable for some businesses – and individuals – than others. The best types of business for running from home are those that are small and office-based – or based predominantly on clients' premises – rather than those that require workshops and machinery or selling directly to the public.

# chapter 5

## Choosing your business idea

And so we come to the nitty-gritty – what business will you start? For some people the answer to this may be obvious. If you are a skilled car mechanic, bookkeeper, photographer or website designer, for example, starting a business within your field of expertise is likely to offer you by far the best chances of satisfaction and success. If, however, you don't have a special skill or interest to base a business around, you will need to give this decision some careful thought.

There is a huge range of home-based businesses you could run. They can be roughly divided into five main categories:

*Professional* – Computer programmer, graphic designer, accountant, architect, personal tutor, interior designer, etc.

*Creative* – Writer, photographer, artist, desktop publisher, sculptor, etc.

*Service* – Childminder, introduction agency proprietor, private investigator, proofreader, indexer, babysitter, upholsterer, carpet cleaner, etc.

*Craft* – Woodworker, toy-maker, picture-framer, french polisher, jewellery-maker, and a range of other craft-based occupations.

*Physical* – Window cleaner, gardener, personal fitness trainer, builder, odd-job (wo)man, car cleaner/valet, curtain-maker, etc.

Of course, any attempt to categorise in this way is somewhat arbitrary. Creative workers such as photographers and artists also have to use physical skills and provide a 'service' to their clients. Likewise, many people in businesses listed above under 'Service' (e.g. childminding and proofreading) quite reasonably regard themselves as professionals as well. Nevertheless, this basic division may help set you thinking about the range of businesses you could start and what type might suit you best. In addition, Chapter 24 lists over fifty different home-based business profiles, with descriptions of each and recommended resources for finding out more.

Your choice of business is entirely up to you, though. For many people, starting their own business based on skills acquired through working for an employer is both a logical and an attractive proposition. On the other hand, if you do not enjoy your work and wish to do something different to make a living, clearly you will need to look elsewhere.

A hobby or interest has provided the basis for many a successful business. Gardening, photography, craft work and working as tourist guide are all examples of businesses which could arise from this source. Of course, you may need to improve your skills and knowledge before you can ply your trade for money – but in most fields there are courses you can take which will (given a modicum of aptitude and ability on your part) bring you up to a professional standard.

Even if you don't have a hobby or interest you could develop into a business, there are still plenty of options open to you. Many popular home-based businesses require basic skills which can be acquired relatively easily: household cleaning, babysitting, window cleaning, pet boarding, commission selling, renting a room, and so on. Or you may be able to learn a skill from scratch by taking a course. Interior design, financial advice work and many alternative therapies are examples of businesses you could start after completing a period of study and passing the relevant examinations. Both open learning and standard courses in these and similar occupations are widely available. Though if you choose this path you may have to wait a bit longer before you are able to get your business up and running – a period of years in some cases.

## Other Considerations

Of course, personal preferences are not the only considerations that come into play here. Other things you will need to consider include:

*Your health* – If your physical health is poor, it is likely to be a mistake starting a business that involves regular strenuous effort, e.g. window cleaning. You must be honest with yourself here. Yes, a healthy outdoor business might help build up your stamina – but if, due to ill-health (perhaps brought on by over-exertion), you keep letting your customers down, you will soon have no business left. If health is a factor, you may be better considering an indoor, office-based business, even if this is not your ideal preference.

*Your aptitudes and abilities* – Again, be honest with yourself here. You might like the idea of being a freelance photographer or writer, but have you really got what it takes to succeed in these competitive professions? For example, it would probably be a mistake to try to launch a career as a freelance writer if all your work has ever received is rejection slips. If appropriate (and possible), get your work appraised by an independent expert, ideally someone who is already successful in your chosen field. This person should be able to give you objective feedback on your abilities and highlight any areas in which you need to improve. Do not rely on encouraging comments from friends and family: they will inevitably view your work through rose-tinted glasses, and in any event are unlikely to be aware of the standards required by professionals in your field. Of course, if you are really determined to make a go of your chosen occupation, you should not necessarily be deterred if you get an unfavourable response initially. This may, however, indicate that it could be wise to spend some extra time polishing and developing your skills before you start to rely on them for an income.

*Your other commitments* – For many people a major attraction of starting a home-based business is that they can combine earning a living with their other domestic commitments. But this in turn, of course, imposes restrictions on the type of business you can run. If you need to be at home to look after young children or an elderly relative, for example, you cannot start a business that requires you to work in other people's houses much of the time, e.g. gardening or household cleaning. Similarly, you may only be able to work at certain times, or need to be free at short notice. These requirements will also have a major impact on the type of business you may be able to run.

*The market* – Whatever the type of business you decide to start, unless there is a large enough group of people willing to pay you for it ('a market') your venture is doomed to failure. Realism, once again, is all-important here. You may have spent your whole life perfecting your skills in producing life-sized wood-carvings of British waterfowl, but how many people will want to buy them and for what price? How will you bring your product or service to the attention of potential buyers – and will it be worth your while to do so for what they are prepared to pay? You must think long and carefully about your proposed business and how you will make money from it. This matter is further discussed in Chapter 6, *Market Research*.

*How much capital you have* – Some businesses (e.g. manufacturing) require relatively large amounts of capital to get started, to pay for such things as special equipment, raw materials, stock, transportation, operating licences, advertising, and so on. Others (e.g. window cleaning) require very little in the way of capital expenditure. Bear in mind, however, that even in a 'low cost' business you will still need to have sufficient funds to cover your needs and those of your family while your business is becoming established. Financial considerations are further discussed in Chapter 11, *Raising Finance*.

*How much you need to earn* – Some (a few) home-based businesses can bring in £100 or more an hour, while in others you will be fortunate to earn this amount in a day. If your business is intended to provide a second income – to augment a pension, for example – then earnings may not matter especially to you. In this case you may simply wish to start a business doing what you enjoy, even if it will never bring in a fortune. By contrast, if your business will have to support a family (not to mention a mortgage, car, foreign holidays, school fees and so on), you will need to zero in on those opportunities that offer the best potential for such an income.

Whatever you decide to do, it is important that it meets all your requirements. If you start a business that is unsuitable, for whatever reason, you will not enjoy doing it. And if you cannot do it properly the business is most likely to fail, thus undermining your self-confidence, and perhaps preventing you from doing something else that you could do well.

## Narrowing Down the Choice

Having read this far, you may well have a number of ideas for businesses you could run. How then can you narrow this down to select the opportunity that would be best for you?

When making this decision, as mentioned above, you will need to take into account a range of considerations, both business and personal. Business considerations include the amount of capital needed to start the business and its earning potential, while personal considerations include your aptitudes and abilities, domestic responsibilities, health, and so on. To work out which idea might be the best for you, write down now your favourite business ideas (up to six) on a piece of paper. Then make another, separate list of everything you require from your venture. To give you an idea, your list might include items such as the following:

- regular hours
- flexible hours
- can be operated part-time
- no night work
- no need to employ others
- low start-up cost
- involves meeting people
- does not involve personal selling
- little paperwork
- no heavy lifting

- involves working outdoors
- involves travelling
- low risk of failure
- high level of profits
- will exploit existing skills
- can be combined with family responsibilities
- will provide potential for expansion

Now look at your list and decide which are the most important requirements for you personally, and which the least. Give each requirement a weighting (a numerical score) to signify its importance, on a scale from one to ten. For example, if the most important item on your list is 'low start-up cost' you might give this a weighting of nine or ten. An item you consider of lesser importance might rate five or six, while an item of relatively little importance might merit a weighting of just one or two.

The next step is to rate each of your own business ideas against the weighted requirements. Taking each business idea in turn, award it points on a scale from 0 to 10 for each of your requirements. Give high points if the idea meets the requirement well, and low points if it does not.

When you have finished scoring each business idea, multiply the points you have awarded it on each requirement by the weighted importance factor. For example, if you have given the idea a score of eight on low start-up cost and the importance weighting you gave for start-up cost was seven, then the total score is 7 x 8 = 56 on that requirement. The overall score for each business idea is then obtained by adding together all the total scores for that idea. The example below should make this clear.

## EXAMPLE

To illustrate this method, take the example of George. A single man in his late twenties, he has recently been made redundant by his employers since he left school, a printing company. As part of the settlement he receives a lump sum payment, and decides to put this towards starting a home-based business of his own.

George wants a business that will provide a steady living doing something he enjoys. His interests include gardening and DIY, and he would like to apply these skills in his new business if possible. Although he has a lump sum to invest, he is keen to make his money stretch as far as possible. He realises that, although he does not have a family to support, he will still need to live off his redundancy payment until the business is operating successfully, and he doesn't want to run up too many debts initially.

While he has no objection to making a fortune, George's greater priority is finding a business with good long-term potential and low risk of failure. He enjoys meeting people, and wants work which will give him the opportunity to do this. He wants to work outdoors at least some of the time. He also likes the idea of working flexible hours, though he attaches less importance to this

George's list of weighted requirements therefore looks something like this:

| Requirement | Importance weighting |
|---|---|
| Low risk of failure | 10 |
| Low start-up cost | 8 |
| Applies hobbies/interests | 8 |
| Chance to meet people | 6 |
| Outdoor work | 5 |
| Flexible hours | 3 |

After careful consideration George has come up with a shortlist of three potentially suitable business ideas. These are:

1. Gardening
2. Window cleaning
3. 'Odd Job' service

Using the scoring method explained above, George's ideas come out as follows.

| Requirement | Importance | Gardening | | Window cleaning | | 'Odd Job' Service | |
|---|---|---|---|---|---|---|---|
| | | Points | Score | Points | Score | Points | Score |
| Low risk failure | 10 | 8 | 80 | 8 | 80 | 7 | 70 |
| Start-up cost | 8 | 7 | 56 | 9 | 63 | 8 | 64 |
| Hobbies/interests | 8 | 9 | 72 | 3 | 24 | 9 | 72 |
| Meet people | 6 | 7 | 42 | 7 | 42 | 8 | 48 |
| Outdoor | 5 | 9 | 45 | 9 | 45 | 5 | 25 |
| Flexible hours | 3 | 6 | 18 | 5 | 15 | 7 | 21 |
| **Totals** | | **313** | | **269** | | **300** | |
| Maximum possible score | | 400 | | 400 | | 400 | |
| **% of total possible score** | | **82.50** | | **67.25** | | **75.00** | |

In this example, the business that is best suited to George's requirements appears to be the gardening service: it scores higher than the other two, and meets over 80% of his requirements.

As a guide, your highest scoring business should meet well over 50% of your requirements. If it does not, you may be advised to look at some other ideas, or re-consider your requirements.

This exercise should help you clarify which business would suit you best. It does have a few shortcomings, however. For one thing it is based entirely on your own views of what the business would entail, and these may or may not be accurate. In addition, the exercise can only help you decide which business might best meet your personal requirements. It will not tell you whether that business is likely to be a success.

Nevertheless, while the result of this exercise should not be taken as gospel, it does provide a reasonably objective way of comparing one idea with another.

## If You Still Can't Decide...

It may be now that you have come down to a choice between two or three different ideas. Each has its attractions but also its drawbacks, and you really can't decide between them. What more can you do to help reach a decision?

One suggestion – which is worthwhile even if you have already decided on a business – is to find out more about what each of your possible businesses would involve in practice. See if you can get part-time or temporary work in a similar field. If this proves impossible, speak to others already doing this type of job, or go and watch them at work. Once you have more information, you are very likely to find yourself re-grading your business ideas against your list of requirements.

Depending on your proposed business, perhaps you could even try starting up in a small way yourself, working in your spare time initially without giving up your main job. This can provide an excellent opportunity to see how you enjoy doing the work, and may also give you a better idea of how much demand there is likely to be for your services.

Overall, the more information you can obtain about your proposed business before you decide to proceed, the better is the chance that it will meet your expectations and requirements.

# chapter 6

## Market research

For your business to succeed, one essential requirement is that there are enough people who will want to buy your product or service. If there are not, all the planning and preparation you put in will be in vain. In addition, if you hope to borrow money to finance your business, any potential lender will want to see that you have given careful thought to who your customers will be. Market research is the means by which you establish this.

## Who Will Be Your Customers?

Think for a moment about your proposed business – what kind of person is most likely to be a customer? It is very unlikely that your answer to this question will be 'anyone'. If you plan to run a car valeting or repair service, for example, your first answer might be 'car owners'. If you thought about it a little more you might add such things as 'car owners who live no more than five kilometres away' and 'car owners who don't have the time, the inclination or the skills to do the work themselves'. Already you have begun to exclude large numbers of people who are not car owners, not DIY enthusiasts and do not live locally, and in so doing started to focus your attention on those people who will be your potential customers.

If your answer to the question above really is 'anyone', then you need to think very carefully about how viable your proposed business is likely to be. If you plan to offer something needed and bought by everybody – soap, for example, or writing paper – the likelihood is you will be entering a marketplace already dominated by big firms. Because these companies produce and sell in huge quantities, their production costs are low. They can also afford to operate on very low profit margins (that is, to sell their products at only slightly more than it costs to make them). Furthermore, such companies usually spend large amounts on advertising. New businesses attempting to break into this market will have to do the same and more if they are to establish themselves and compete effectively with the existing companies.

Few small businesses have the resources to compete in such a marketplace. Rather, what you will need to do is find a gap, or niche, in the market where you can sell your product or service to a particular group of customers at a price that allows you to make a reasonable profit. The purpose of your market research will be to find such a niche in the market.

## Segmenting the Market

As mentioned above, for a small, home-based business, trying to sell to everybody is unlikely to bring success. You need to find a smaller group of people who could be interested in the product or service you plan to offer. Having identified such a group, you will then have to decide what products or services to offer these people, how to bring your offer to their attention, and how to persuade them to buy.

Segmenting the market is the term used to describe the process of dividing the whole population into a number of separate market 'segments'. These segments are groups of people with something in common. Once you have identified a particular segment (or segments) as your potential customers, you can start to design your marketing plan – that is, your plan for turning these people from potential into actual customers.

There are many ways of segmenting markets, and it is up to you to decide which methods might be most relevant for your business. Some of the most common methods are listed below.

*(1) By geographical location*

This will be relevant for many small businesses serving a local community. You might decide to segment the market into potential customers living within (say) a 3 km radius, a 10 km radius and a 20 km radius. For many products and services people prefer to buy locally if they can, as this saves them time, effort and (usually) money.

*(2) By age*

You could segment the market into children, teenagers, young adults, parents, middle-aged people and older people. Each of these groups might have different requirements. If you plan to offer a mobile hairdressing service, for instance, you may need different approaches according to whether you wish to appeal to young, fashion-conscious people or to older people with more traditional requirements

*(3) By type of customer*

There are many ways of segmenting the market by type of customer. Often, these will be specific to the business concerned. In the case of a private investigator, for example, you could segment your potential market into solicitors, local authorities, companies and private individuals. Another way of segmenting by type of customer – when selling craft items, say – would be into retailers, wholesalers and end-users. Each of these potential markets would need to be treated differently. Retailers and wholesalers would expect credit terms, for instance, while private customers are generally prepared to pay immediately.

Other ways of segmenting the market include by gender, occupation, religion, income level, leisure interests, car ownership, marital status, family size and so on. Understanding the nature of the people in your target market segment is vitally important when you are trying to sell to them. For example, an office caterer providing food and drinks for a predominantly middle-class workforce might need to offer quite a different range of products from a mobile snack bar in the middle of a factory estate.

Any of these forms of segmentation can be further segmented. For example, you could sub-divide private vehicle owners into car owners, van owners, motorbike owners, and so on; and these groups themselves could be further sub-divided into Ford owners, Nissan owners, etc. The purpose of this is to find one or more market segments which will (you hope) provide the customer base for your new business. You will then be able to plan every aspect of your business with these people in mind.

To be attractive to your business, a market segment should ideally have the following qualities:

(1) There are enough people in it to make serving the group profitable.
(2) The segment is growing, or at least stable, rather than shrinking.
(3) There are unsatisfied needs among this group of people which the business could profitably meet.
(4) There is not so much competition among existing firms that another operator would be unable to attract a sufficient share of the market.

Your market research will help you discover the size, level of competition, and profit potential of particular segments. Having completed the research, and clarified the make-up of your chosen groups, you then face a choice:

(1) You can ignore the differences between segments and try to develop a product or service which concentrates on meeting the needs of a wide range of potential customers, OR

(2) You can recognise the differing needs of people in different market segments, and try to offer a range of products or services tailored to meet as many as possible of these, OR

(3) You can recognise the differing needs of people in different market segments, but choose to offer a narrow range of products or services concentrated on no more than a small number of chosen groups.

None of these strategies is necessarily better than any other, and each may be appropriate at a different stage in your business's development. When starting out, however, (3) is often the best strategy for gaining a foothold in the market, so long as there are sufficient potential customers in that particular market segment.

## Why Do People Buy?

As well as identifying who will be your potential customers, another important question to be addressed by your market research is 'Why will they buy?' The reason for this is not hard to see. Unless you know what your potential customers are looking for, how can you be sure you will be offering what they want?

If your business will involve making and selling a product, for example, your customers may fall into two main categories, retailers and private individuals. In the case of the former, the most important factors in determining whether they will buy from you are (a) whether they think your products are likely to sell, and (b) how much profit they will make from each sale. Private individuals, by contrast, may have a wide range of reasons for buying a particular product, including:

- cost
- perceived value for money
- appearance (including colour, shape, design, etc.)
- reliability
- quality
- performance
- delivery time
- safety
- reputation/recommendation of others
- image (for example, the product is associated in the customer's mind with being young, successful, glamorous)

With service businesses, likewise, people may have a wide range of reasons for buying. In the case of a gardening service, for example, a customer might buy for any (or all) of the following reasons:

- wish to save time and effort
- age/poor health/disability
- wish to get professional results
- recommendation of neighbours
- seen the gardener's work elsewhere
- inexpensive
- good value for money
- convenient
- trust/liking for the individual concerned
- range of services on offer

The reasons people have for buying one product or service rather than another are not always the obvious, logical ones; they may, for instance, prefer to do business with someone local, or an older person, or someone they like the look of, rather than a competitor who fails to meet these criteria. It is essential, therefore, to find out what people in your target market really want from the product or service you plan to provide. Knowing this, you will then be better placed to decide exactly what to offer, and how to market your business to make it most attractive to your potential customers.

## Doing the Research

Market research is essential to identify who will be your customers and find out something about their requirements. But how do you go about doing this in practice? A wide variety of market research methods is available. They can be roughly divided into 'desk research' and 'field research'.

### Desk research

Desk research, as the name suggests, is research you can do without leaving your desk – or, at most, by means of a trip to the local library. You can obtain a surprising amount of useful information by this method alone. Some of the most useful sources include:

*Directories* – There are directories listing the major companies in most trades and industries. The best-known UK publications include Kompass, Key British Enterprises and Kelly's – all of which nowadays have a strong Internet presence as well (see below). These directories can give you invaluable information about the size of a particular market, the main players, and potential customers and suppliers. Clearly, such directories will be less useful if you plan to run a local service business (e.g. window cleaning); but in cases where you will be selling your services to other businesses (e.g. writers, computer programmers and graphic designers) they can provide invaluable information about the sector concerned.

*Government information/statistics* – The government, via a privatised company The Stationery Office (TSO), publishes research findings and statistics covering such matters as population changes, industrial production, imports and exports, and so on. These are obviously less useful for finding out about local trading conditions, but can provide valuable information on overall trends.

*Trade magazines, newsletters and journals* – There are national and international publications serving almost every trade and occupation, from Toy Trader to PR Week, Homebrew Supplier to Construction Weekly. These can provide invaluable information on trends and current issues in the business area concerned. As well as reading the articles, look at the advertisements. They can tell you a great deal about potential suppliers, customers and competitors.

*Competitors' literature* – This is perhaps the most useful source of all. By studying the advertising material produced by your competitors you can learn a lot about whom they see as their target market and how they sell to them. Not only that, you can learn from any mistakes they make and adapt some of their better ideas yourself!

And finally, don't neglect the mass of invaluable information on the Internet. Specialist search engines such as Kellysearch at www.kellysearch.co.uk – the online arm of Kelly's Directories, mentioned above – make searching for UK company or product information quick and simple.

In addition, many small businesses in every sphere nowadays have their own websites, and this can provide a quick and easy method for checking out the competition. If you plan to start a childminding business, for example, enter 'childminding' in a search engine such as Search UK (www.searchuk.com). This will lead you to a number of websites advertising childminding services, as well as a range of organisations serving and representing childminders both locally and nationally.

*Field Research*

While desk research can provide useful background information about the area of business you plan to enter, much of this is bound to be fairly general. To get specific information about potential customers and their requirements, you will almost certainly need to do some practical 'field' research as well.

A lot of this can be informal. If you plan to start a local service business, for example, ask around your friends, neighbours, colleagues and relatives. Find out who (if anyone) they employ at present for the service in question, and the reasons they have for using them. Ask them if they have any complaints about their present supplier, and if there are additional services they would like which this person does not at present provide. Ask what it would take to persuade them to switch to a new supplier. Other informal research methods include talking to people already in similar businesses (maybe in other parts of the country or offering different services, so they will not see you as a potential competitor); observing other businesses; and using your own personal judgement – what would YOU require if you were a potential customer?

Researching potential competitors, as mentioned earlier, is also essential. If possible, obtain copies of the sales literature produced by these businesses. You could also try contacting them, posing as a potential customer, to find out their prices, procedures, sales methods, and so on. This may seem a little underhand if you have no intention of buying, but the information you can obtain in this way is invaluable – and you may be certain that, once you are in business, others will do just the same to you. Once you have obtained this information, try completing the simple exercise below.

## EXERCISE

### Researching Your Competitors

Start by identifying the three other businesses who will be your main competitors (if you can only identify one or two, just use these). Write the name of each business on the top of a sheet of paper, and put below it, in a few sentences, where the business is located and the products and/or services it sells. Also include here any information you have been able to obtain about the prices they charge or their hourly rates.

Now, for each of these businesses, write down (a) the business's particular strengths, and (b) any weaknesses you have been able to discern. For example, with a shop, the strengths might include friendly service and a prime high street position, while weaknesses might include high prices or a limited range of goods.

Finally, for each of these businesses, list as many advantages as you can think of which your business will have over them. To give you an idea, these might include a wider range of products or services, free delivery, a 24-hour emergency service, free initial consultation, money-back guarantee, expert advice, and so on.

---

This exercise should help you to clarify who will be your main competitors and how you will encourage people to buy from you rather than from them. It is worth continuing this exercise even when your business is up and running. For one thing, the other businesses, if they start to lose customers to you, are quite likely to try to win them back by offering extra benefits themselves. It is a good idea to keep a file or folder on each of your main competitors, and, as well as your observations about them, put in copies of their advertising leaflets, price lists, order forms and so on.

If you are going to sell a product via retailers (or wholesalers), you can also approach them for help and advice. They will have a good knowledge of what their customers want, and should be able to tell you what does and doesn't sell. This approach will not work if you plan to sell directly to end users, of course.

Finally, if you really want to do your research properly (and impress any potential lender or backer) you could consider doing a small-scale survey. This involves contacting a good cross-section of people who might be your customers (not just friends and colleagues) to find out what they want and what influences them when deciding what to buy. One good way of doing this is by producing a simple questionnaire. Questionnaires are important tools in market research, and worth looking at in more detail.

## Questionnaires

The only way to get accurate information about people's needs, views and habits is to ask them. Questionnaires (written lists of questions) provide a planned and structured way of doing this. Using a questionnaire ensures that you ask everybody the same questions, and makes it much easier to compare and analyse the replies. There are a few basic rules to good questionnaire design:

(1) *Keep it short and simple* – Most people will not object to answering a few simple questions, but a multi-page document which will take up hours of their time is quite a different matter. Think carefully about what you need to find out, and ask only the most important things. There should be no more than five to ten questions in total. Wherever possible use yes/no questions and multiple choice (where the person answering has to choose from a list of possible answers), as these are easier to complete and to analyse.

(2) *Don't ask 'loaded' questions* – A loaded question is one which invites a particular answer. If, for instance, you ask 'Would you use my service if it was cheaper than the existing ones', most people will answer 'Yes' without much thought. It is better to ask neutral, factual questions such as 'Where do you have your car serviced at present?' or 'What would you consider a reasonable price for having all your carpets professionally steam cleaned?' The information you obtain from questions such as these will be much more useful to you.

(3) *Don't ask too many 'open' questions* – All questions can be either open or closed. A closed question allows only a limited number of replies – two in the case of yes/no questions, perhaps half a dozen with multiple choice. This makes closed questions quick and easy to answer. By contrast, open questions (such as 'Do you think a mobile

car repair service is a good idea?') admit a huge range of possible answers.

Occasionally open questions may produce interesting and unexpected replies, which can affect your whole thinking about the business. But they can also lead to lengthy discussion and debate, and replies to them can be very difficult to compare and analyse. For that reason, it is normally best to have no more than one or two open questions on your questionnaire.

(4) *Ask the right people* – there is no point in talking to people who are not going to be potential customers. Finding the right people may require house-to-house interviews or stopping people in the street. It will also depend on the type of business you plan to start. For example, if you hope to start a desktop publishing service, you will need to talk to people in local small businesses who are likely to be your main clients.

(5) *Ask as many people as you can* – The more people you interview, the more useful and accurate your results are likely to be. Rather than try to cram everybody's answers on to one piece of paper, it is best to make photocopies of your questionnaire and complete one for every person you ask. This makes adding up the figures at the end much easier.

## Your Marketing Plan

Once you have completed your market research, you should be in a good position to prepare your marketing plan. This will set out how you propose to attract customers for your business (and, as already noted, without customers no business can survive). Specifically, your marketing plan should answer the following four questions:

(1)  How will you advertise your product or service?
(2)  What other forms of promotion will you use?
(3)  How will you sell your product/service (e.g. retail, wholesale, agents)?
(4)  What features and benefits will you emphasise when trying to attract customers?

Let's look at each of these in a little more detail.

*(1) How will you advertise your product or service?*

If you are providing a local service, the main places you are likely to want to advertise include local newspapers, directories, magazines, and so on. On the other hand, if you aim to sell nationally – perhaps by mail order – you will need to use national newspapers and magazines, and perhaps other media such as posters, TV and radio. In the latter case your advertising costs are likely to be high, and you might consider using an advertising agent to write and place your advertisements for you. Advertising agents are discussed in more detail in Chapter 22, *Where to Get More Help*.

*(2) What other forms of promotion will you use?*

Advertising is by no means the only possible method of bringing your business to the attention of possible customers and persuading them to buy from you. Some other possibilities include:

- sales promotions (e.g. free gifts or special opening offers)
- taking a stall at an exhibition
- preparing a card or leaflet and distributing them to potential clients
- public relations (persuading the local media that what you are doing is newsworthy and merits free coverage)
- publicity stunts (another way of obtaining publicity and media coverage)
- sponsorship (e.g. persuading the local football team to wear the name of your business on their shirts, in exchange for your practical and financial support)

Advertising and promotion are discussed in more detail in Chapter 17, *Marketing and Selling*.

*(3) How will you sell your product or service?*

You have a range of choices here, depending on the type of business you intend to start. If you are making a product, for instance, you might decide to sell it through shops or wholesalers, or you might try to sell directly to customers yourself. You might alternatively, or in addition, take on an agent and pay him a commission (a proportion of the selling price) for every product he sells.

Each method has advantages and disadvantages. If you sell through retailers or agents, for instance, they will take part of the profit on every sale. On the other hand, if you attempt to sell directly to customers yourself, you are likely to have to spend a lot more time and money on advertising and promotion. The method you choose to sell your products or services will have important implications in areas such as pricing, cashflow and budgeting.

*(4) What features and benefits will you emphasise when trying to attract customers?*

Your market research should have given you some idea of the features people in your target segment are looking for in the products or services you intend to provide. In your marketing plan, you should therefore be able to specify what will be the main 'selling points' you emphasise in your advertising.

## Assessing Market Trends

Identifying potential market segments and the needs of the people in them are essential if your business is to succeed. Markets, however, are constantly changing. If your business is to prosper in the long-term, it is important to avoid relying on a market with poor future prospects. You should be especially wary of starting a business based on providing goods or services that may be merely a fad, with demand liable to collapse when the next fashion takes over.

Obviously it is impossible to predict how exactly the world will change in the future, but when planning your business it is important to try to take into account not only what the marketplace is like today, but how it may be in five, ten or twenty years time. Market research can be invaluable for spotting and predicting future trends, which can affect even apparently stable occupations such as gardening. For example:

- The growing number of elderly people in the population could lead to an increase in demand for lawn mowing and basic garden care services.

- More people taking foreign holidays in exotic locations might lead to a greater demand for exotic plants and people skilled in cultivating them.
- The trend for both couples in a relationship to go out to work may mean they have less time for activities such as gardening and be more inclined to employ a part-time gardener.
- With more and more people going on the Internet, there is likely to be a growing demand for computing courses for beginners, installation and repair services, and so on.

There is, of course, a positive side to all this as well. Social changes – more widespread car ownership, for example, or people living longer – can bring new opportunities for far-sighted businessmen and women who anticipate such changes and prepare for them.

# chapter 7

## Planning permission and business rates

The good news is that most home-based businesses do not require planning permission. The rules say that permission is not required provided your work use 'does not change the overall character of the property's use as a single dwelling'.

So a graphic artist or website designer (to take a couple of fairly random examples) working in a spare bedroom would not in most cases require planning permission. The same applies even in the case of small-scale manufacturing and service businesses – for example, making toys or craft items, or carrying out clothing alterations and repairs. Planning permission is not normally required so long as your activities do not affect the overall domestic character of the building. If, however, the non-residential use ceases to be subsidiary, perhaps because your business has expanded, planning permission will be required for a change of use. A planning authority might consider the following evidence that a material change of use has occurred:

- a significant alteration to the appearance of the dwelling
- a significant increase in volume of visitors or traffic
- a significant increase in noise, fumes or smell
- the installation of special machinery or equipment not normally found in a dwelling
- the laying out of rooms in such a way that they could not easily revert to residential use at the end of the working day

In practice, the attitude of the planning department is likely to be influenced by any negative comments they receive from your neighbours. It follows that an important consideration is how much disruption your business activities are likely to cause. If you know your business is likely to be noisy or create fumes or some other nuisance, you may need to think about ways in which you could reduce the nuisance to your neighbours. A freelance musician might have to consider adding sound-proofing to her practice room, for example.

If you need to physically extend your property to accommodate your business, you almost certainly will need planning permission. A full discussion of the planning laws is outside the scope of this book, but broadly in England and Wales you will need permission for new building work if:

- For a terraced house (including end of terrace) or any house in an official conservation area, the volume of the original house would be increased by more than 10% or 50 cubic metres (whichever is the greater).

- For a detached or semi-detached house, the volume of the original house would be increased by more than 15% or 70 cubic metres (whichever is the greater).

- In any case, the volume of the original house would be increased by more than 115 cubic metres.

There are also certain other stipulations. For example, you must apply for planning permission if (irrespective of the points above) the addition would be nearer to any highway than the nearest point of the original house, unless there would still be at least 20 metres between the house as extended and the highway.

Applying for planning permission involves contacting the planning department of your local authority (their number will be in the phone book), and obtaining and completing the necessary application forms. You will also have to pay a fee. In addition, you are likely to require building regulations approval from the local authority's building control department – though your chosen contractor will normally handle this on your behalf. One final point is that you should check the conditions in your mortgage or lease, as this may place conditions on uses to which the property may be put. If you are in any doubt about what you may or may not do, it is advisable to consult a solicitor.

## Business Rates

If you are running a business from home, your local council may take the view that you are liable to pay business rates in addition to your normal council tax. This is an area that is shrouded in confusion, however, with different councils adopting different policies. Considering that some 60% of all new businesses are now started up at home, there is an urgent need for clarification on this point from the government.

In general, the situation at present appears to be that if you are working from your kitchen table or a desk in your bedroom, you are unlikely to be adjudged liable to pay business rates. If you have a dedicated home office, however, you may be. And if, for example, you build an extension solely to house your business, you almost certainly will have to pay business rates. In that case you will need to contact the business rates section of the council so that they can assess how much you will have to pay.

If you want to avoid paying business rates in addition to your normal council tax, the best advice is probably to avoid setting aside a room in your home solely for use as an office. If the room can still be used as a spare bedroom, for example – perhaps you keep a camp bed in the corner – there is a good chance you will escape liability for business rates.

If you set up your business as a limited company (see Chapter 8, *Forms of Business Organisation*), it is best to have your company registered at another address, e.g. that of your accountant. In that case, you will be regarded in law as an employee of the company who just happens to be working from home. Your situation will be no different from someone working at home as an ordinary employee (as many thousands of people now do). This can actually be a major advantage to setting up as a limited company.

Finally, if you are going to work from home, it is good practice to notify your mortgage provider. They are unlikely to have a problem with this, unless you are turning your home into commercial premises, e.g. a shop. As stakeholders in your property, however, they would normally expect to be kept informed.

# chapter 8

## Types of business organisation

Even if you only want to run a small home-based business on your own, you should know something about how businesses generally are organised. There are three most common forms of business organisation:

(1) Sole trader
(2) Partnership
(3) Company with limited liability

Each of these types of organisation has its advantages and its disadvantages. It is impossible to say which is best, because none is best in all circumstances.

## Sole Trader

This is the oldest, simplest and most common form of business organisation. It is also the most straightforward to set up. Basically, the owner or proprietor of the business is the business. Whether you trade under your own name or use a business name such as Garden Designs, you are solely responsible for everything the business does. Being a sole trader does not mean you cannot employ anyone – it simply means that you are the only owner of the business (often called the proprietor). This form of organisation is common in small service businesses of all kinds.

Operating as a sole trader is simple and cheap. It also has the great advantage that all the profits belong to you personally, so if your business does well you can make a lot of money. There are other benefits as well. A sole trader makes all the decisions himself, so this type of business can be very flexible, adapting quickly to changing circumstances. If, for instance, your customers start asking for new products or services, you can make the changes needed to provide them quickly and easily. There is no-one to argue with you if you wish to alter the way the business is run. Without doubt, operating as a sole trader can provide great personal satisfaction.

Being a sole trader does have its drawbacks, however. Just as all the profits of the business belong to you, so you personally are responsible for all its debts. If the business cannot pay its creditors, you, the business owner, can be made bankrupt – that is, you may be forced to sell your personal possessions, your house, your car, and so on to pay off the business's debts.

As a sole trader, you are liable not only for what you do, but for what your employees (if you have any) do as well. For instance, if they fail to install or repair an electrical appliance correctly and it causes an injury, you personally may be sued. It is therefore essential that you insure against such mishaps. The business is also heavily dependent on your good health, and you should insure against the possibility of this failing.

Most sole traders operate businesses that do not require substantial amounts of capital (money invested in the business). They largely provide their own money at the beginning. However, when the time comes to expand, the owner may have to borrow in order to increase the assets of the business, and this is where other people may enter the picture.

It is at this stage that one of the other forms of business organisation may be considered, because they make more money available. However, they do involve a reduction in personal control and direction of the enterprise.

## Partnership

In this form of business there are two or more owners. They divide the profits between them, and also share liability for any debts that arise. Partnerships are common in all fields where personal service is involved. Many professional practices such as accountancy, law and medicine are organised in this way.

A great advantage with a partnership is that there is usually more money available to be invested in the business. The worries and responsibilities are shared among more people and, of course, there are more people to contribute to the business's success. Everything does not depend on one person. If one partner is ill, or just wishes to take a holiday, the whole business will not come grinding to a halt.

A big disadvantage of a partnership is that if it fails you can be called upon to pay all the debts of the partnership. This includes the debts of your partners if they cannot pay their share – even if the debts were incurred without your knowledge.

In addition, there tend to be stricter legal requirements governing partnerships, and this means more rules concerning how you organise and run the business. Responsibility for decision-making will be shared between you and your partners, thus also reducing your freedom of action, and perhaps leading to disagreements.

Furthermore, partners will often put different amounts of money into the business. In some cases, one partner may have supplied most of the money, while the other has brought the expertise. This may cause disagreement over how profits should be shared. It would not be reasonable for profits to be shared simply in proportion to money invested; the partner who put up less money would naturally expect some reward for his expertise, though deciding what this should be might be difficult. It is essential that such issues should be settled at the start in a formal partnership agreement. If you are thinking of starting a business as a partnership, you should certainly seek legal advice.

## Company

A company – properly called a joint stock company – is where a group of individuals put their money together to make a 'joint stock' of capital. The people who put up the money are called shareholders. They all own a share of the company, and expect to receive a share of its profits.

The shareholders are also called 'members' because they are part of the company, but the company is a legal entity quite separate from the members who own it. In law, a company is regarded as an individual in its own right: it can make a profit or a loss; it can be held responsible for the actions of its employees; it can be sued; and, if the worst comes to the worst, it can go bankrupt (though in the case of companies this is called 'going into liquidation').

The amount of the company each shareholder owns is directly proportional to the money he puts in. The shares of large companies are bought and sold on the stock exchange. Such companies are called public companies, and anybody can buy their shares through a stockbroker or bank. The shares of many smaller companies, however, are owned entirely by the people who work in them.

### Limited liability

Nowadays nearly every joint stock company in the world is formed on the principle of limited liability. In the UK such companies must put the letters 'Ltd' (the abbreviation for Limited) or PLC (short for Public Limited Company) after their name. In other parts of the world they put letters like 'S.A.', 'N.V.', 'GmbH' and 'Inc'. These are all very similar in meaning.

Limited liability means that if a company fails and has to close down, the individual shareholders will not be held responsible for the company's debts. Each shareholder only loses the money he spent on buying his shares. Unlike a sole trader or a partner, his personal possessions cannot be sold to pay the company's debts; his liability is limited to the amount he invested (hence the term 'limited liability').

Because of the principle of limited liability, establishing your new business as a company may appear an attractive option. Potential lenders and creditors are very well aware of the principle and its implications as well, however. If you apply for a loan or credit terms, they will naturally want to ensure that their money is returned in the event of your company failing. Particularly if you are setting up a new business, therefore, they may require you to personally guarantee any debts, e.g. by allowing them to place a legal charge on your property. In this case, if your company does subsequently fail, the creditor can still pursue you personally for any debts outstanding.

*Company directors*

Although a company is regarded in law as a separate person, it cannot carry out any business by itself. People must be appointed to manage and run the business, and these people are called the company directors.

In a small company, such as a family business, the shareholders are often themselves the company directors; they both own the company and run it. With larger companies it is usual for shareholders to appoint directors with the necessary skills to manage the company on their behalf. The shareholders meet just once a year, at an annual general meeting, to express their approval or disapproval of the way the directors are managing the business; to appoint new directors if required; and to accept or reject the directors' recommendations on how the profits are to be distributed.

Again, in a small company all or most of the directors will be closely involved in the running of the business. In a larger company many of the directors may only work part-time for the company, simply attending board meetings at which general policy decisions are taken. They leave the day-to-day running of the company to one director, known as the managing director, or a small number of executive directors. Unless they are also shareholders, directors are not entitled to a share of the profits. However, they are entitled to a fee for the work they do for the company, plus their expenses. The managing director and executive directors, who work full-time for the company, also receive a salary, just like any other employee.

The directors may employ staff to work for them and managers to supervise those staff, but the directors have the overall responsibility and are answerable to the shareholders for the success or failure of the enterprise. The shareholders have the right to demand not only that the directors act in good faith, but also that they exercise skill and care in managing the business.

## Which Type of Organisation?

Each type of business organisation has its advantages and disadvantages, and you must choose the type that is most suitable for your needs.

The sole trader approach is likely to be the first choice for many small home-based businesses. Its advantages are:

(1) It is easy to set up
(2) The owner has complete personal control
(3) All profits belong to the owner personally

The disadvantages of being a sole trader are:

(1) The liability of the owner is unlimited – he may be made personally bankrupt if the business fails.
(2) The growth of the company is limited by the amount of money the owner either has or can borrow as a personal loan.
(3) If the owner is ill, the business may not be able to carry on; although sometimes a good employee may be able to manage the business for a short while.

Setting up in partnership can overcome some of the above drawbacks. A partnership is more complicated to set up than a sole trader business, but less so than a limited company. The advantages of a partnership are:

(1) It offers greater scope for financial investment and growth.
(2) It allows the skills of several people to be combined, rather than relying on one person.
(3) If one partner is ill, the others can continue the business; the business may also continue on the death of one partner.

The disadvantages are:

(1) As with a sole trader, the liability of the partners is unlimited; however, in this case, the partner accepts liability not only for his own decisions but for those of his partner or partners. It is therefore essential that a partnership is only entered into with people whose integrity and ability can be relied upon.

(2) Although there is likely to be more money available for a partnership than for a sole trader, there will generally be much less than for a limited company.

(3) Each partner has less direct control than a sole trader.

A limited liability company is the safest type of enterprise, but it is also the most complex. Its advantages are:

(1) No individual is liable to the company for any amount in excess of the value of his shares; thus, everyone knows how much he is committing himself to from the start.

(2) If the company fails, individuals will not normally face personal bankruptcy and the loss of their property and possessions.

(3) The amount of money available for investment is much greater than with other forms of business.

(4) More expertise is generally available.

The disadvantages are:

(1) The business is more complicated to set up and will generally require the professional services of a lawyer and an accountant.

(2) There is a cost involved in registering as a legal company.

(3) The person who sets up the business does not own it – no individual does. He may well be the majority shareholder (that is, the person who owns most of the shares) and have a considerable amount of control, but he cannot have the complete personal control of the sole trader. What he does will be subject to the power of other shareholders, and to the requirements of very strict laws.

One other advantage of operating as a limited company, mentioned in the last chapter, is that if you have your company registered at another address, e.g. that of your accountant, you will be regarded in law as an employee of the company who just happens to be working from home. This can help to avoid problems regarding planning permission, liability for business rates, and so on. Your situation will be no different from someone working at home as an ordinary employee, something many thousands of people now do. This can be a major advantage to setting up as a limited company.

In summary, each type of business organisation has both advantages and disadvantages. Many people starting out opt for sole trader status, and perhaps subsequently expand into partnerships and companies as their businesses grow and develop. When starting out, the important thing is to decide what type of organisation will be most appropriate for your business. If you decide to start off as a sole trader no special action as needed, though you should of course notify the Inland Revenue and Department of Social Security (see Chapter 15, *Tax, National Insurance and VAT*). If you are considering setting up in partnership or as a limited company, greater formalities are required. In this case it is highly advisable to obtain professional advice from a solicitor and/or an accountant (see Chapter 22, *Where to Get More Help*).

# chapter 9

## Your business name and image

One essential decision you need to make before you start trading concerns your business's name. An obvious possibility for one-person businesses is simply to use your own name. Using this alone, however, tells people very little about what you do. Many businesses take advantage of this opportunity to explain their activities and project a sales message. A simple approach would be to use your name, and add a word or two about the business – for example, Pete Martin Investigations or Rehman Curtains & Upholstery.

You can also use your business name to express your product or service's main selling point. For example, if you are running a children's entertainment service with conjuring tricks, you might decide to call yourself 'Magic Parties'. If you are a plumber offering a 24-hour emergency service, you might choose the name 'Instant Plumbing'.

Avoid choosing a very long name, as people will have difficulty remembering it. Another reason is that you will have to answer the phone in your business's name. Saying 'Littleton Vehicle Cleaning and Valeting Service' twenty or thirty times a day could soon have your tongue in knots! A simple, easy-to-pronounce name, no longer than three or four words, is usually best.

There are some words you may not use in your business name without official clearance. In Britain, such words include 'royal' and 'authority'. If you are in any doubt about the legality of the name you wish to use, a solicitor should be able to advise you.

Finally, you should try hard to avoid giving your business the same name as another that is already trading. If the other business thinks you are using their name to cash in on goodwill they have built up with their own customers, you could end up in court accused of 'passing off'. This could happen even if you copy the other business's name unintentionally. The local phone book should reveal whether another business in the area is already using your proposed name. You could also make enquiries at your local chamber of commerce.

## Your Business's Image

Your business's name is one aspect of its image: the way your business appears to other people and the impression they get of it. Often this goes beyond purely factual matters to feelings and emotions: for example, a business's image may be young and dynamic, or safe and traditional; witty and creative, or honest and straightforward. Apart from the business's name, another important contributor to your image is your letterhead and logo (if you have one).

Most businesses have to send letters to people such as customers and potential customers, suppliers, banks, government officials and so on. Your letterhead is, literally, the heading you use for this. A suitable letterhead can help to give your business the kind of image you want. Just as when choosing your business name, therefore, you should give careful thought to the design of your letterhead.

Letterheads are usually printed on white paper. Tinted papers, such as cream and pale blue, are also popular but may be a little more expensive. Weight of paper is usually measured in grammes per square metre (gsm). Eighty gsm is about the minimum for a letterhead, and if you want your image to be an up-market one you may prefer to use a weight of 100 gsm or more.

One other decision you will need to make concerns the colour of the printing. Black is cheapest and photocopies well. Full-colour letterheads can look impressive, but cost more to print. If you want colour on your letterheads, consider using just one or two colours, perhaps on tinted paper to give the effect of an extra colour. Finally, if you have a computer/word processor, you can of course design a letterhead on this and print it out either in colour or black-and-white (depending on your printer). Modern word processing and desktop publishing programs can give excellent results, but you may need to spend a little time experimenting in order to get a finished effect you like.

Your letterhead will need to include most or all of the following:

- the name of your business
- your address
- your telephone number
- your mobile number
- your fax number
- Your e-mail address
- Your website URL

If you are using a business name other than your own, it is customary to include your own name as well – e.g. at the foot of the page, 'Proprietor: J. Johnson' or 'Managing Director: Michael Smith'. This helps people who may be contacting you for the first time by giving them a name they can ask for. Limited companies are required to provide a range of information on their letterhead, including company registration number and country of registration.

One other thing you may decide to include on your letterhead is information about the business and/or an advertising slogan. For example, you could include details about the products or services you supply, and a short sales message: 'Photos to remember', 'Keeping your garden green', 'Builders of excellence', or whatever.

Your letterhead may also include a logo. This is a symbol or emblem you hope people will come to associate with your business. Large companies spend sizeable amounts designing and publicising their logos, and there is no doubt that they can make a valuable contribution to a business's image. For small, home-based businesses logos are probably less useful. But if you have a good idea for one, by all means use it if you can. The present author, for example, has on his letterhead a stylised typewriter image originally obtained from a copyright-free artwork disk.

If you can't, or don't want to, design your own letterhead, most printers will do this for you, or you may wish to commission a graphic artist (see Chapter 22, *Where to Get More Help*). It should be possible to adapt your letterhead for use on business cards, compliments slips, invoices and so on. In addition, if your business has transport, such as a van, a version of the letterhead and/or logo should appear on this also. The overall aim is to create a clear, distinct identity for your business in people's minds, so that whenever they see the name, letterhead or logo, they will be know instantly to whom it refers. This is part of what large companies call their corporate image. Even if yours is just a one-person home-based business, there is no reason why you cannot do likewise!

# chapter 10

## Business plan and financial forecasts

So far we have been examining various matters that must be taken into account before starting a home-based business. These aspects are brought together in an important document called your business plan. This is the document that sets out, in words and figures, all the plans you have made for starting and running your business.

Preparing a business plan is far from being a mere academic exercise. Your business plan will fulfil three important functions:

(1)  It will help you clarify and organise your thoughts.
(2)  It will help you raise finance.
(3)  It will help you monitor your business once it has started.

Let's look at each of these in a little more detail.

*(1) Organising Your Thoughts*

When you are planning a business there are so many different things to consider that it is very easy to become confused. Putting the whole thing in writing can help you clarify your thoughts and assess the whole project more objectively. In addition, to complete the plan you will have to answer a lot of questions. This forces you to go out and do the necessary research to find answers, which in itself is an excellent discipline.

*(2) Raising Finance*

If you need to apply for a loan, your business plan will demonstrate to the bank manager or lender that you have carefully considered every aspect of the proposed business, and that you know exactly how much money you need to borrow and what you will require it for. This will help reassure him that his funds will be wisely used. Even if you do not plan to apply for a loan, a business plan could help save you from losing your own money.

*(3) Monitoring Your Progress*

The business plan sets down the path along which the business should be moving. When you first start your business there will be a vast number of things to do, and it is easy to delude yourself that you are doing well simply because you are busy. Your business plan – in particular the cashflow forecast – will guide you through this period. With the plan at your side, you can take stock at regular intervals (every month perhaps) of how your business is doing. If you are failing to meet your targets, you can then decide on what remedial action to take...and the sooner the better!

## Style and Presentation

Business plans can be set out in many different ways, though the information contained is much the same. Some general guidelines are given below.

(1) Your plan must be neatly and professionally presented. It should be typed or word processed (never handwritten) and enclosed in a cover or binder that includes the name of the business and the name and address of the person (or persons) behind it. If an accountant has been closely involved in preparing the plan, his or her name and address should be given as well.

(2) The plan should be written in the third person – that is, 'the proprietor' or 'Mr/Ms Rogers'. You should avoid referring to yourself in a business plan as 'I' or 'me'. This is simply about appearing business-like.

(3) The plan should be as concise (i.e. brief) as possible, whilst including all the necessary information that a financial backer or other interested party would want to see.

(4) The text should avoid too many salesman's phrases such as 'this wonderful product' or 'this incredible opportunity'. The tone needs to be confident but objective. Rather than make wild claims and sweeping generalisations, in a business plan, as far as possible, you should stick to facts you can prove.

(5) The plan should clearly demonstrate the viability of the proposed business. Remember that potential backers will be looking for evidence of two things in particular: market research, and financial planning and control.

## The Contents

Your business plan will need to include most or all of the following sections.

- Introduction
- Product or Service Details
- Personnel

- Market Research and Marketing Plan
- Premises, Equipment and Transport
- Suppliers and Sub-contractors
- Legal Aspects
- Financial Information
- Risk Assessment
- Appendices

Let's look at each of these in a little more detail.

*(1) Introduction*

This is where you explain the nature of the business and its proposed structure (e.g. sole trader, partnership, limited company). It should be no longer than one or two paragraphs. If the plan has been written for a specific purpose – e.g. to support an application for a loan – this should also be mentioned here.

*(2) Product or Service Details*

In this section you describe in some detail the product or service you will be providing. If it is a product, you should show clearly how it will be made, explaining all the stages involved. If instead you are providing a service, you need to explain precisely what this is and what type of customers you expect to require it.

*(3) Personnel*

In this section you include information about the person or people who are behind the business and will be managing it. If you intend to be a sole trader, this will of course be yourself. In partnerships and limited companies, it will also include your partners or fellow directors.

You should describe briefly your past work experience, especially where this is obviously relevant to the new business. Include any educational or occupational qualifications, and any previous experience of running a business. You should also mention here any business-related training you are undertaking. If you are receiving active advice and support from a business development agency (for example), state this here also. Your overall aim is to demonstrate to a potential lender or backer that you, as the person behind the business, are well prepared for self-employment, and have the experience and training to make it a success.

Finally, in this section you should mention whether you intend to employ any staff. You should indicate how many you will need, what skills they will require, how much you expect to have to pay them, whether they will be full- or part-time, and what training they will need.

*(4) Market Research and Marketing Plan*

This is a very important section that will normally take up at least a page of text, and in many cases more. Its purpose is to convince the reader that there will be enough demand for your product or service to make the business viable within the market in which you intend to operate.

This section should therefore summarise your market research, and in particular answer the following questions:

(1) Who will be your customers, and what will be their requirements?
(2) How large will your potential market be?
(3) Who will be your competitors – their names, addresses and details.
(4) What are the main strengths of these competitors?
(5) What will be your advantages over them – or, to put this another way, why will people buy from you rather than them?

All your answers should be backed up with facts and figures from your market research. When you are describing the market size, for instance, you should explain clearly how you have arrived at this figure. Statements such as 'There is considerable demand for...' or 'Many people require...' are worthless without some market research data to back them up.

Also in this section you should describe your marketing plan. This concerns how you will advertise, promote and sell your product or service. Specifically, it should answer the following questions:

• How and where will you advertise your product or service?
• What other forms of promotion will you use (e.g. direct mail, exhibitions, telephone selling)?
• How will your product or service be sold (e.g. wholesale, retail or through agents)?

Marketing is further discussed in Chapter 17, *Marketing and Selling*.

*(5) Premises, Equipment and Transport*

This section will state the premises to be used. For most readers of this book this will be their home, so you should state this, with perhaps a few words on why this is ideal for your purposes (low cost, convenience, etc.). If you will be working from an office in your home, or perhaps a converted garage or shed, this should be mentioned as well. Remember, the aim is to convince backers that working from home is a sensible option for your business and you have all the facilities and space required.

Similarly with equipment and transport, you should explain what you need, how it will be obtained – e.g. by leasing, hire purchase or outright payment -and whether it will be new or second-hand. If you will require a lot of equipment, it may be worth including more details in the Appendix.

*(6) Suppliers and Sub-contractors*

Many businesses rely on other businesses to supply them with raw materials, components or services. Any problems in obtaining these can result in disaster for the business, especially if it is a new one. In this section you should therefore explain who your main suppliers and subcontractors will be and why you have chosen them, stating alternatives where possible. You should also comment on any discussions you have already had with suppliers, agreements reached, credit facilities negotiated, and so on.

*(7) Legal Aspects*

In this section you should include details of any legal matters or requirements which may impinge on your business. For example, if your particular business requires a permit or a licence, you should state here how this will be obtained, what it will cost, what delays are likely between applying and receiving it, and what are the criteria you and the business will have to meet to qualify.

Also in this section you might mention patents (where you are making an original product and wish to prevent others copying it), planning permission (where such permission is required to operate your proposed business), and so on. It is most important that your business fulfils all the legal requirements before you start trading, and backers will want to see that you have taken this into account.

*(8) Financial Information*

This is probably the most important part of the whole business plan, because it must demonstrate to potential lenders that you have a clear plan and targets for your business's finances, both now and over the coming months. Specifically, it will show that you know how much money you need, what you need it for, how much you expect to receive and to pay out during the business's first twelve months, and how much margin for error you have given yourself.

This section should also explain your policy on pricing. With products you should state the mark-up you intend to use, while for service businesses you should state your hourly rate (for more details, see Chapter 16, *Pricing Your Services*). It is customary to mention the normal mark-ups or hourly rates of your particular industry, and give the reasons if yours differ from this. This is very important, as new businesses often under-price, often with dire results.

The section should also include a cashflow forecast (see below). This shows the expected flow of cash into and out of your business – especially crucial in the first few months. With all financial projections you should avoid being over-optimistic and allow reasonable amounts for contingencies (especially overheads, which always seem to be larger than anticipated). You should also state any assumptions you are making, e.g. concerning credit you are given by suppliers and have to extend to customers.

*(9) Risk Assessment*

In this section you will discuss the risks that are attached to your project, and how you propose to control them. Every business carries some element of risk, and any potential backer will want to see evidence that you have taken this into consideration. Potential risk could come from a number of sources:

- a competitor setting up near you
- a major customer going into liquidation or taking his business elsewhere
- your main supplier or sub-contractor ceasing to trade
- customers taking longer than anticipated to pay their bills
- a long-term decline in demand for your product or service

- lower than expected levels of sales
- changes in the law making your product/service harder to sell
- increases in taxation
- variations in interest rates
- variations in foreign exchange rates (where the business is involved in trading with other countries)
- accident or illness
- flood or fire

In this section you should explain the main risks your business is likely to face, and how you intend to monitor and control them. You should also comment on any contingency plans you have to meet setbacks, such as who will take over if you are ill.

*(10) Financial Requirements*

This is a crucial section, especially when the plan is being used as part of a funding application. Here you state clearly the total capital the business requires, how much you (and your partners/fellow directors) are putting in, what loan will be required, how much share capital (where the business will be a limited company), and what overdraft facilities, if any, you may need. Where you are applying for a loan, you should also state here what security you can offer (e.g. your house, or a friend/relative who will act as guarantor).

*(11) Appendix*

A variety of things may be enclosed in the Appendix at the back of the plan. They may include:

- CVs (Curriculums Vitae) of the people behind the business
- alternative cashflow forecast showing the effect of reduced sales
- other financial information, e.g. break-even analysis, operating budget, projected profit-and-less account and projected balance sheet
- detailed product information and technical data (where appropriate)
- detailed information about equipment and machinery
- detailed market research information
- correspondence or agreements with potential suppliers and customers
- sales literature, leaflets, photos and so on

## Cashflow Forecast

As mentioned above, the cashflow forecast is an essential component of any business plan. The purpose of the cashflow forecast is not to predict the profit (or loss) your business will make. Rather, it is concerned with predicting the flow of cash in and out of the business. Cash is the life-blood of any business, and failing to pay attention to this essential element is one of the commonest reasons for business failures. By assessing the predicted flow of cash into and out of the business, you can:

- identify possible cash shortages before they occur and take action to avoid them
- identify times when you may have surplus cash, and ensure it is used efficiently
- ensure that cash is always available when required, e.g. for paying staff wages
- encourage more efficient methods of using resources and saving costs
- and make soundly-based decisions about your business

A cashflow forecast lists month by month your business's predicted income and expenditure, and shows your net financial position (i.e. how much you will have in the bank) at any time. The cashflow forecast is especially important in the early days of your business, as it will enable you to see how much money you are likely to need in the early months before you start to receive a steady flow of income from your clients. An example cashflow forecast for a part-time home-based business is shown in *Figure 1*. The exercise below will help you draw up a cashflow forecast of your own.

| Month | Pre-start | 1 | 2 | 3 | 4 | 5 | 6 | Total |
|---|---|---|---|---|---|---|---|---|
| Capital from proprietor | 500 | | | | | | | |
| **Income** | | | | | | | | |
| Business cards | | 75 | 162 | 188 | 200 | 200 | 175 | 1000 |
| Personal stationery | | 200 | 250 | 300 | 300 | 300 | 400 | 1750 |
| Other printing | | | | 50 | 50 | 100 | 200 | 400 |
| **Total income** | **500** | **275** | **412** | **538** | **550** | **600** | **775** | **3650** |
| **Payments** | | | | | | | | |
| Start-up costs | 100 | | | | | | | 100 |
| Stock of paper/cards/envelopes/chemicals | | | 70 | 95 | 110 | 120 | 140 | 535 |
| Heat & light | | | | 62 | | | 62 | 124 |
| Telephone | | | | 63 | | | 63 | 126 |
| HP repayments | | | 50 | 50 | 50 | 50 | 50 | 250 |
| Wages for proprietor | | 400 | 400 | 400 | 400 | 400 | 400 | 2400 |
| Insurance premium | | 10 | 10 | 10 | 10 | 10 | 10 | 60 |
| **Total payments** | **100** | **410** | **530** | **680** | **570** | **580** | **725** | **3595** |
| Net cash flow | 400 | (135) | (118) | (142) | (20) | 20 | 50 | 55 |
| Opening balance | 0 | 400 | 265 | 147 | 5 | (15) | 5 | |
| Closing balance | 400 | 265 | 147 | 5 | (15) | 5 | 55 | 55 |

Figure 1. A simple cashflow forecast prepared for a part-time home-based printing business.

## EXERCISE

This exercise is designed to help you prepare a cashflow forecast for your proposed business. Obviously at this stage many of the figures will be estimates, but try to be as accurate and realistic as you can. Use only whole figures, rounding up or down as appropriate. The table below is shown for six months to fit on the page, but you should copy it and extend it to cover the first twelve months of trading. If any of the categories does not apply to your business leave them out (e.g. packaging costs may be incurred by people making products but not by those offering a service). Some rows have been left blank for you to put in categories of expenditure specific to your particular business.

## Cashflow Forecast

| | Month | 1 | 2 | 3 | 4 | 5 | 6 |
|---|---|---|---|---|---|---|---|
| | **RECEIPTS** | | | | | | |
| 1 | Sales – cash | | | | | | |
| 2 | – debtors | | | | | | |
| 3 | Loans received | | | | | | |
| 4 | Capital introduced | | | | | | |
| 5 | Other receipts | | | | | | |
| **6** | **TOTAL RECEIPTS** | | | | | | |
| | **PAYMENTS** | | | | | | |
| 7 | Cash purchases | | | | | | |
| 8 | Payments to creditors | | | | | | |
| 9 | Proprietor's Drawings | | | | | | |
| 10 | Staff wages | | | | | | |
| 11 | Capital items | | | | | | |
| 12 | Transport | | | | | | |
| 13 | Packaging | | | | | | |
| 14 | Rent/rates | | | | | | |
| 15 | Loan repayments | | | | | | |
| 16 | Overdraft interest | | | | | | |
| 17 | Professional fees | | | | | | |
| 18 | Advertising | | | | | | |
| 19 | Postage & stationery | | | | | | |
| 20 | Telephone | | | | | | |
| 21 | Heating/electricity | | | | | | |
| 22 | Insurance | | | | | | |
| 23 | | | | | | | |
| 24 | | | | | | | |
| 25 | | | | | | | |
| 26 | | | | | | | |
| 27 | Sundries | | | | | | |
| **28** | **TOTAL PAYMENTS** | | | | | | |
| 29 | NET CASHFLOW | | | | | | |
| 30 | OPENING BALANCE | | | | | | |
| 31 | CLOSING BALANCE | | | | | | |

To help you complete the form, here are some notes together with the item number they refer to.

*Line 4* – This shows any money which you or your partners or fellow directors are putting into the business as permanent capital.

*Lines 7/8* – These are for payments you make to suppliers for stock or materials. Cash payments are made immediately and included on line 7. Payments to suppliers who allow you credit facilities are shown on line 8. Remember that, in a cashflow plan, all payments are shown in the month when they are actually made, not when the debt is incurred.

*Line 9* – This is money drawn from the business for the personal use of the proprietor or (in the case of partnerships) proprietors.

*Line 11* – This refers to the purchase of capital items such as equipment or machinery. Note that in the budget forecast the cost of such items may be spread over a period of years using depreciation, but in a cashflow forecast they must be shown when they are paid for.

*Line 17* – Includes such things as accountant's fees, legal fees, and so on.

*Lines 23-26* – Include any other items appropriate to your business.

*Line 29* – To calculate NET CASHFLOW, deduct TOTAL PAYMENTS (line 28) from TOTAL RECEIPTS (line 6). This will show you the extent to which the total amount of cash in the business has increased or decreased during the month concerned. In the first few months it is quite likely that payments out will be greater than receipts, so the calculation will give you a minus figure. Using the normal accounting convention, such figures should be shown in brackets, e.g. (1250).

*Line 30* – This shows the amount of cash you have at the start of the month. It is the same as the closing balance of the previous month (line 31).

*Line 31* – The closing balance is the amount of money you have at the end of the month. It is the opening balance plus or minus the net cashflow (line 29).

When completing your own cashflow forecast, follow this simple procedure:

(1) Use a pencil, rather than a pen, so that you can make changes and corrections easily.

(2) Work ACROSS the sheet, starting at the top with sales – that is, estimate your cash sales for each of the first twelve months you are operating, then income from debtors.

(3) Miss out line 3 at this stage, but fill in lines 4,5 and 6, still working across the page.

(4) Next, fill in lines 7 to 28, missing out for the moment lines 15 and 16.

(5) Subtract line 28 from line 6 to get the NET CASHFLOW (line 29). Complete this for the whole year.

(6) Now calculate the opening balance (line 30) and the closing balance (line 31) for every month. In the first month the opening balance will be zero and the closing balance will be the same as the net cashflow. In subsequent months, the opening balance will be the same as the closing balance of the previous month, while the closing balance will be the opening balance plus or minus that month's net cashflow.

(7) When the tasks above have been completed, you will almost certainly have a number of negative figures in line 31. If this is the case, you will need to borrow money to keep your business afloat. Looking at the chart, try to estimate how much is negative for a long-ish period (six months or more), and how much is negative for a shorter period. The long negative part can then be met by a loan, while the shorter part can be bridged with an overdraft (see the next section Raising Finance). If there are NO negative figures in line 29 you will not need a loan or overdraft, and lines 3, 16 and 17 will all remain zero.

(8)  Put your loan requirement into line 3, and check that the sum of that amount and the overdraft does not exceed your line 4, since lenders normally prefer not to put more money into a project than the proprietor. If the figure you need to borrow considerably exceeds the amount you have available to put into the business, you may need to consider forming a partnership or a limited company to raise extra funds.

(9)  Finally, assuming the requirement in (7) has been met, put the loan repayments and/or overdraft fees in lines 16 and 17, and re-calculate the totals accordingly.

Having worked out exactly what your business's financial requirements are likely to be, we can now move on to the important topic of raising finance.

# chapter 11

## Raising finance

Whatever the type of home-based business you plan to start, you will need to find some money to finance it. Part of this will be needed to cover the cost of equipment and materials, and part to cover your own living costs until the business is bringing in a regular income. You will need to establish whether you can raise all this money yourself, or whether you will need to obtain a loan (or grant) for some of it.

To do this, you will need to calculate how much capital you yourself can raise. When working this out, remember to include the value of all of the following.

- cash
- savings
- stocks and shares
- your car
- insurance policies which can be cashed in
- any other material possessions which could be sold (e.g. jewellery)

From this you will need to deduct:

- any other outstanding loans
- any bills due for payment

This will give you a figure for your total net worth. Of course, this is just a theoretical maximum, and it may neither be necessary nor desirable to put all this money into the business in practice. For example, if you have an old car, it may be more valuable to you and your business as a means of transport than whatever price you could sell it for. If you redeem a life insurance policy early, you may end up receiving a very poor return for the money you have paid in. The same applies if you sell stocks and shares at the wrong time (i.e. when the price is low). Nevertheless, if you really do need to raise the maximum possible, the calculation will give you some idea of how much this would be.

## Capital Requirement

Having worked out the maximum you could raise, you must now compare this with the total amount of money you will need to start your business – your capital requirement. Once you have done this, you will be able to make plans for how you will bridge the gap.

Your capital requirement will be made up of two things. These are:

(a) *Permanent capital* – This is money needed for the purchase of equipment, vehicles and so on which will become permanent possessions of the business, otherwise known as fixed assets. For many businesses the largest fixed asset they require is premises. Clearly this will not be an issue with a home-based business!

(b) *Working capital* – This is money needed to meet the day-to-day running costs of the business. Running costs include such things as printing, postage, stationery, telephone bills, raw materials, and so on.

Running costs also include the money you need just to cover your own living expenses. Often this is more than you might think. To work out how much you need just to survive, complete the exercise below.

## EXERCISE

### Personal Survival Budget

Cost Per Month

Mortgage/rent
Loan interest
Local rates/taxes
Water
Gas/electricity/oil
Telephone
Life insurance
Other insurance
Pension
Food
Clothing
Travel/car
Holidays
Subscriptions/newspapers
Children
Other items
Unexpected contingencies

TOTAL:
LESS any other family income:
SURVIVAL INCOME:

This is the minimum you need every month just for you and your family to survive.

In working out your initial capital requirement, you need to take into account both permanent capital and working capital. Once your business is running successfully, your working capital needs should be covered by the income the business is generating, and perhaps by short-term borrowing such as a bank overdraft. In the first few months, however, the business is unlikely to be receiving much income, and you may need to find most of your working capital from other sources.

## Raising Money From Other Sources

Having calculated (1) how much capital you can raise, and (2) how much you need to start the business, you should now have a good idea of how much money you need to find from other sources. Knowing this figure is important, because it will have a considerable bearing on how you proceed next.

If you need to raise a relatively large proportion of the total, and this money is required for investment in fixed assets such as a computer, vehicle or special equipment, your need is for permanent, long-term capital. While you may be able to raise some of this by means of a loan through a bank or other financial institution, you might also need to find a backer or partner willing to provide capital which will be permanently invested in the business. This may mean that you form a partnership or limited liability company with other participants, rather than operating on your own as a sole trader.

On the other hand, if your needs are proportionately small and the finance is required mainly for working capital (as will be the case with most home-based businesses), you may be able to negotiate the necessary bank overdraft facilities to cover these, while finding most of the permanent capital yourself. In this case, you may choose to operate as a sole trader to keep complete personal control of the business.

## Raising Finance

It is no disgrace if you find you need to borrow some money when starting out. Few businesses are able to operate solely on the owner's funds. Those who try frequently fail because they are undercapitalised (that is, they do not have sufficient capital to meet their working requirements). Most businesses have to borrow to some extent. What is generally needed is:

(a) a mixture of long-term and short-term finance, and
(b) a balance between what is provided by the owner of the business and what by outside lenders

Borrowing needs to be matched with the purpose it is required for. That is to say, if you need money for a short period only, you should apply for short-term finance such as a bank overdraft (this is an agreement with your bank that, over a short period, you can draw out more money than you have in the account, so long as you later pay the money back to the bank with interest). On the other hand, when funds are required for long-term purposes – say the purchase of a vehicle or computer equipment – a long-term loan is likely to be more appropriate.

Different types of finance are suited to different purposes. For example, it would be a mistake to buy expensive machinery with a ten-year lifespan using short-term finance such as a bank overdraft. For one thing, over ten years you would pay much more in interest charges than with a long-term loan; and for another, by doing this you would be tying up a valuable source of short-term finance for things such as working capital. This is summed up in a well-known piece of advice for businessmen: **Don't borrow short to pay long.**

So far as the balance between your own and outside finance is concerned, as a rough guide most financial institutions will expect you to put up at least half the total cost of any business venture. The exact amount they will be prepared to lend you is governed by a range of factors, including the type of business you intend to start, your past business and financial record, how much security you can offer against the loan, and so on.

**Types of Finance**

There are three broad categories of finance, short-, medium and long-term. Let's look at each of these in turn.

*(1) Short-term finance (up to one year)*

This is normally used for such things as:

- financing seasonal/cyclical fluctuations in trade
- financing general working capital requirements
- purchasing minor fixed assets with a short working life
- providing temporary, bridging finance while long-term finance is arranged

There are many potential sources of short-term finance. The most common are listed below.

*Overdrafts* – a bank overdraft, already mentioned, is the most popular form of short-term finance. Overdrafts have the advantage of being simple to set up, and are also very flexible. Generally speaking, the bank specifies a maximum you are allowed to borrow up to, and you can use as much or as little of this as you require. On the other hand, interest rates for overdrafts are generally higher than for medium or long-term loans, and they are repayable on demand. This makes them unsuitable for long-term borrowing.

*Trade credit* – most suppliers are willing to extend credit terms to business customers. That is to say, they will allow customers a certain period of time – thirty days perhaps – from delivery before requiring payment. In effect, therefore, this is a short-term loan. If you go beyond the agreed period, however, interest may be charged and, ultimately, trade terms may be withdrawn.

*Hire purchase* – this is a way of purchasing items by instalments. By paying an initial deposit and regular sums over a period of time, a business acquires ownership of the goods. The business has use of the goods from the initial deposit, but they do not officially become the property of the business until the final instalment has been paid.

*Leasing* – this is a method of financing the use of an asset rather than its actual purchase. It is used by businesses to finance things such as motor vehicles, computers, photocopiers and machinery. The leasing company retains ownership of the items, and charges the business a rental for their use. Leasing finance may be short- or medium-term, according to the duration of the lease.

*Factoring* – this is a popular source of short-term finance for established businesses. Companies known as 'factors' take over the business's trade debtors in exchange for an agreed reward (usually a percentage of the amount outstanding). This means that the business has the use of money owed to it immediately, and does not have to spend its time pursuing overdue accounts. As mentioned, factors are only concerned with taking over a business's trade debtors, so this form of finance will not be of interest if you are just starting out.

*(2) Medium-term finance (1-5 years)*

This is normally used for financing fixed assets with medium-term life such as cars and computer systems, and meeting increased working capital requirements. It may also be used to replace a persistent overdraft.

The main source of medium-term finance is bank loans, which are usually repaid by monthly instalments. Loans may be made at a fixed interest rate, where the amount of each repayment is fixed at the beginning of the loan and cannot alter; or at a variable rate, where the interest rate can go up or down according to economic conditions, with monthly repayments varying accordingly. Fixed rate loans make budgeting easier; but if interest rates generally fall, there is a risk of getting locked into a situation where you are paying for your loan at a rate which is no longer competitive. Bank loans are typically given over a period matching the expected life of the asset they are to purchase.

*(3) Long-term finance (over five years)*

Long-term finance is used for financing major fixed assets with a long life and for providing semi-permanent working capital. The main sources of long-term finance are bank loans, mortgage loans and equity finance (share issues). Most home-based businesses are unlikely to require long-term finance when starting up, though it may become relevant if you subsequently decide to expand, perhaps into specialist business premises.

## Applying for Finance

If you need extra finance beyond what you can raise yourself, you will probably need to apply to a lending institution such as a bank or finance house. Such institutions are in business to lend money, but will not of course give you a loan just because you ask for it. A lender will want to ensure that his (or his depositors') money will be wisely used, and returned with interest in due course. He will want to see a business plan showing that you have thought out every aspect of your proposed business, and a cashflow projection showing your anticipated financial situation and requirements.

In addition, the lender will want to assess you personally, trying to assess how well or badly you will run your business. He will look at such things as:

- your character, background and previous experience
- your previous financial history, how thrifty you have been, and how you have handled any existing accounts you may have
- what funding you require: what type of finance you are looking for, how much, and for how long
- how much you are prepared to put into the project (he is likely to be looking for a substantial contribution, probably matching that from the bank)
- how and when the borrowing will be repaid
- what security you can put up in the event that you default on repaying the loan

Obviously, not all potential borrowers will be able to meet the banks' ideal, and many loans are made to people who fall short of this – particularly to those with a sound business proposition, but lacking a track record in business. In borderline cases, the lender has to rely on his personal judgement.

When applying for finance, it is therefore important to present a smart, businesslike image. Even if you are nervous inside, you need to appear well-prepared and confident (though not over-confident) about your business and its prospects. As mentioned, you will also need to present a business plan showing you have taken into account every aspect of your proposed business.

## What Happens if You Can't Get a Bank Loan?

If you have a good case for funding and present it (and yourself) well, there is every chance that you will succeed in your funding application. If you are turned down, however, you may need to re-think some of your plans. Basically you have two possible courses of action.

One is to reduce your capital requirements, for instance by starting part-time or reducing the range of services you offer initially. Once a lender can see that you are trading successfully, he is likely to be much more willing to provide a loan. Alternatively, you may be so successful working this way that the profits generated mean you no longer need extra money at all!

The other solution is to find an alternative source of finance. Various organisations exist to provide help and support for people starting businesses of their own, and some can also help with loans or even grants. Depending on your age and background, the area where you live and the type of business you plan to start, any of the following organisations may be well worth approaching.

*1. The Prince's Trust Business Programme* – The Prince's Trust Business Programme helps unemployed young people between the ages of 18 and 30 in England and Northern Ireland start businesses of their own. They offer low-interest loans of up to £4,000 (up to £5,000 for a partnership), and grants of up to £1,500 in certain circumstances, subject to local availability. They also offer test-marketing grants of up to £250, again subject to local availability. Each successful applicant is also allocated a mentor to help with all aspects of setting up and running their business. For more information, call the Prince's Trust on 0800 842842, or see their website at www.princes-trust.org.uk. Applicants aged 18-25 in Scotland should contact the Prince's Scottish Youth Business Trust on 0141 248 4999, or see their website at www.psybt.org.uk. The Prince's Trust does not currently offer loans or grants in Wales.

*2. Regional Development Agencies (RDAs)* – There are nine Regional Development Agencies in England, whose role includes promoting economic development and regeneration in the regions concerned. Especially if you live in a deprived urban or rural area, they may be able to assist you with loans, grants and other forms of business support. Note that they will certainly want to see your business plan before offering you any money. The best way to find the Regional Development Agency covering your area is to check on the RDAs national website at www.englandsrdas.com, or you can phone their national secretariat at 020 7222 8180.

*3. Business Link* – Business Link is a government-funded service designed to promote enterprise in England. Business Link services are delivered by local Business Link organisations, and managed by the Regional Development Agencies (see above). They provide support, advice, services and information to anyone planning to set up a business in their area. While they do not normally offer grants or loans, they will certainly be able to let you know of possible sources of finance locally. To be connected to your nearest Business Link centre, simply phone 0845 600 9 006. Alternatively, see the national Business Link website (which also has a searchable grants directory) at www.businesslink.gov.uk.

4. *Other National Business Support Services* – As stated above, Business Link only covers the regions of England. If you live elsewhere in the UK, the following are the organisations to contact.
*Scotland: Business Gateway* – 0845 609 6611 – www.bgateway.com
*Wales: Business Eye* – 08457 96 97 98 – www.businesseye.org.uk
*Northern Ireland: Invest NI* – 028 9023 9090 – www.investni.com

5. *Chambers of Commerce* – Chambers of commerce provide their members with training, business support and finance. They also have extensive libraries containing information on marketing and looking for trading partners. For more information on your local chamber of commerce and what it can offer, phone their national office on 024 7669 4484, or see their website at www.chamberonline.co.uk.

6. *Business Angels* – If you have an original idea that you think could make a lot of money, it may be worthwhile approaching a business angel. In return for investing in your business they will expect a share of future profits and a say in how the business is run, so it is important to choose someone with whom you believe you will be able to build a good working relationship. Contact the British Business Angels Association on 0207 089 2305, or via their website at www.bbaa.org.uk.

7. *'The Dragons' Den'* – This popular BBC TV programme lets aspiring entrepreneurs bid for funding from wealthy businessmen and women. In exchange for their investment, the so-called dragons will normally expect a portion of the equity in your business, but this means you do also get the benefit of their expertise as well. Even if your bid is unsuccessful, the TV exposure can help generate interest in your venture. This is obviously speculative – but if you have an original business idea or invention and need extra finance to bring it to market, there is no reason not to try it. You can apply via the BBC website at www.bbc.co.uk/dragonsden.

8. *Your Local Council* – All local councils offer advice and practical support for people in their area starting new businesses. Typically these will include a range of publications, advice on legal matters such as licensing and rates, and practical support such as low-cost start-up units. They may also be able to provide grants and loans in suitable cases. Look at the page for your local council in your phone back. The phone number you require for more information may be listed under Business Services or Economic Development.

If you are still unable to come up with the cash you need, another option (mentioned earlier) may be to bring in a partner or partners, either to help you with the day-to-day running of the business or simply to provide finance in exchange for a share in the profits (a 'sleeping partner'). Or, of course, you may have a friend or relative who would be prepared to lend you the money so long as it is repaid (with interest) once the business running successfully.

If, however, none of these approaches proves fruitful, and starting on a smaller scale is not feasible, another option to consider is starting a different business altogether. By starting a less expensive business initially, even if this is not what you ideally want to do, you may be able to raise sufficient capital to finance the business you really do want to run. Many a business has been started on the back of money raised washing cars, doing odd jobs, or (nowadays) buying and selling goods in Internet auctions!

# chapter 12

## Help from the Post Office

Almost anyone running a business from home will need to use the services of the Post Office, and specifically their mail collection and delivery arm, Royal Mail. Indeed, many businesses would be unable to operate without their help. As well as daily postal deliveries and collections, they offer a wide range of special services tailored to the needs of businesses. Below are listed some of the main services which may be useful to you in running your home-based business.

*Private Box:* A private box provides you with a short and easy to remember alternative business address (e.g. PO Box 321). It can be useful if your postal address is on the lengthy side, or if you don't want customers and suppliers to know that you are operating from home.

Mail posted to a private box is held at the local delivery office until you pick it up, or you can pay an extra fee to have it delivered to your usual address. A private box currently costs £60.15 a year or £48.80 for a half-year. If you want your mail delivered to your home rather than going to collect it, you pay basically the same amount again. The total cost in this case is £120.35 a year or £97.65 for a half-year.

*Keepsafe:* If you are going to be away from home for a period of up to two months, you can have your mail held by the post office and delivered on a day of your choice. The Keepsafe scheme costs £8.50 for up to 17 days, £12 for 24 days, £15 for 31 days, and £28 for 66 days. You can obtain an application form from your local post office, or via the Royal Mail website at www.royalmail.com. A week's notice is required.

*Special Delivery:* This is the service to use with urgent and/or valuable items. With their Special Delivery Next Day service, Royal Mail guarantees that your package will be delivered by the next working day in mainland Britain and Northern Ireland, and within three days at most in the more remote islands. Prices start at £4.60 for a single item weighing up to 100g. Royal Mail also offers a Special Delivery 9am service, which guarantees that your package is delivered by 9am the following morning. Prices for this service start at £10.30 for a single item weighing up to 100g.

Compensation is payable if items are damaged or lost (an item being defined as lost if it has not been delivered 10 days after the deadline). The normal maximum compensation is £500 for Special Delivery Next Day and £50 for Special Delivery 9am, but with more valuable items you can opt for a higher level of compensation (up to £2,500) by paying an extra fee at the time you send the package. Special delivery items are handled by a different network from other postal items. You can track their progress and confirm their safe arrival on the Royal Mail's website at www.royalmail.com.

*Business Collection:* If you do a lot of business via the post, you may find it helpful to arrange for a postman to come and collect your outgoing mail from your premises. If you spend over £15,000 a year on postage, the Royal Mail will provide this service free. Even if you do not spend this amount, however, they will collect your post for a fee. This is £450 a year for a daily collection from Monday to Friday, and a further £130 a year if you want a collection on Saturdays. A single, one-off collection costs £10.

*Business Reply and Freepost:* These services allow customers to contact you at your expense. With the Business Reply service, specially printed cards or envelopes (either first or second class) are supplied for customers' use. Business Reply is a good choice when using mailshots or magazine inserts to advertise.

With Freepost, customers reply by putting your Freepost address on their own envelopes. This can be ideal if you want to encourage a good response to local radio or press advertising, but you can also use your Freepost address on printed reply cards or envelopes in mail shots. There is an annual licence fee of £73.40 covering both these services. You then pay an additional 0.5p (compared with the cost of franked mail) per item handled

*Mailsort:* This title covers a range of Royal Mail services which offer discounts of up to 30% for bulk mailings. To qualify, you must post a minimum number of letters (4,000, unless all letters are for delivery in the postcode area from which they have been mailed, when the minimum falls to 2,000), 90% of your mail must be fully and accurately postcoded, and all of it must be sorted and prepared according to Royal Mail's instructions. You can make additional savings if you apply barcodes to your mail. The Royal Mail will advise you on this.

*Household Delivery Service:* The Royal Mail provides a door-to-door delivery service for leaflets, special offers and other promotional material. This can provide a handy, economical way to target potential customers in your area. You can select the addresses to be delivered to according to a wide range of criteria. These include postcode area, district or sector; TV region; geo-demographic (i.e. certain types of property only); residential/business, and so on. Costs vary according to the number and weight of items you are sending.

*Admail:* Admail enables your customers to respond to any address you like. You can use this service if you wish to use a more prestigious address in your advertising, or perhaps somewhere more local to an area you are targeting.

Royal Mail will forward all responses to your home address, or to another destination if you prefer. Your Admail address can be short and therefore memorable, which is useful if you want to use it in advertising. All letters are redirected by first class post. Costs range from £126 for 30 days up to £750 for a year. Discounts may apply if you have more than one contract.

*Franking:* If you send out a lot of post, a franking machine may be a good investment. It will save you time and trouble buying and sticking on stamps, and the results look more professional. In addition, you will save at least 2p a letter compared with standard first- and second-class postage rates. You can either hire or buy a franking machine. More information is available from the Royal Mail Sales Centre on 08457 950 950.

*The Direct Mail Information Service:* The Direct Mail Information Service (DMIS) undertakes regular in-depth research into the direct mail industry in the UK. You can get free outline reports from DMIS on topics such as direct mail trends, customer loyalty, response rates to mailshots, and so on. More information is available from The Direct Mail Information Service, Mail Media Centre, Stukely Street, London, WC1V 7AB, tel. 020 7421 2250. They also have a website at www.dmis.co.uk on which many of their reports can be viewed.

For more information about any of the above services, a good starting point is the Royal Mail Customer Service Centre at Freepost, RM1 1AA, tel. 08457 740740. And, as already mentioned, the Royal Mail website at www.royalmail.com includes details of all the services described in this chapter, and many more.

# chapter 13

## Phones and faxes

Just as most home-based businesses depend on Royal Mail for their smooth running, so too do they rely on having an efficient telephone service. Most home-based businesses depend on the phone for a range of reasons:

- For many businesses this is the most convenient way for customers and potential customers to get in touch.
- You can easily contact suppliers, advertising media, your professional
- advisers, and so on.
- If you have business partners or associates, or employ staff, it will be easier for them to contact you (and vice versa).
- If you want to use the facilities of the Internet to aid your business, you will probably need a phone line to connect with it.
- Likewise, if you want (or need) a fax machine, you will need a phone line to connect it to.

It follows that nearly all businesses need a phone. To save costs you may decide to start off by using your home phone for the business as well. If you do this, however, you will need to brief other family members on how they should answer calls. If your teenage children aren't prepared to sacrifice all their street cred by saying 'Johnson's Window Cleaning Service' whenever they pick up the receiver, simply getting them to state the phone number is a good compromise. In contrast, a laid-back voice saying 'Yeah?' gives a poor first impression, and may result in a lost sale.

Some people are confident and at ease on the phone, while others are at best uncomfortable with it. The best advice if the latter applies to you is to try to relax and be natural, and remember that this form of communication, like all such skills, improves with experience. Always keep a notebook by the phone, so that you (and anyone else who answers) can keep a record of any messages. This is much better than writing on scraps of paper, which can easily be lost.

## BT Network Services

As well as the basic phone service, a wide range of additional services is available from BT (British Telecom). You will have to pay an extra charge for many of these, but this is generally quite modest (typically £1.75 a month). Those services of the greatest potential interest to home-based workers include the following.

*Call Minder* – Call Minder is a network-based answering service. It provides an alternative to having your own answering machine (see below) which may be attractive to some home-based workers. Call Minder will automatically answer your calls when there is no reply or if you are already speaking to someone else (something an ordinary answering machine cannot do). You can retrieve your messages by dialling 1571 from your home phone (free) or, with the use of a special PIN number, any touch-tone phone in Britain or overseas (for which you will have to pay a call charge).

*Call Diversion* – Call Diversion enables you to divert automatically incoming calls to almost any number in the UK, including mobile phones. In addition to the monthly fee, you will be charged for the portion of the call from your home number to the number diverted to. Call Diversion can be useful if you are spending a period of time away from home, say working at a customer's premises. Diversion can be switched on and off at will by entering the appropriate code numbers from your home phone.

*Call Sign* – Call Sign gives you an extra phone number on your line, identified by a different ringing tone. Without having an extra line installed, you can therefore have a separate number to give to clients and in your advertising. When the phone rings, you (and your family) will know by the tone whether it is a business or personal call. You could also use the Call Sign service to identify incoming faxes.

*Caller Display* – Caller Display lets you see who is calling before you pick up the phone, and records details of any callers while you've been out. As well as paying the extra fee for this service, you will need to obtain a special receiver that includes the necessary LCD display panel. These are available from BT and other specialist suppliers.

*Call Waiting* – Call Waiting gently bleeps to tell you that a second call is on the line. You can either put the first caller on hold and speak to the second caller, or end your first call and speak to the second caller. This is a useful service to have if you get lots of phone calls and don't want to lose a potential customer because he can't get through.

*Ring Back* – With this service, if the number you are calling is engaged, you simply dial '5' before you put the phone down. Your phone will then ring as soon as the other person's phone is free (a special ringing tone is used to indicate this). Pick up your phone, and their phone will start to ring. Note that you will be charged a fee each time you use this service.

## Free Services

*Friends and Family* – This free service lets you specify up to 5, 10 or 15 numbers (according to your chosen BT calling plan) you call frequently. You then get a 10% discount when phoning those numbers, which may include international and mobile phone numbers, All or any of your Friends and Family numbers can be changed at any time. Alternatively, you can get BT to select your numbers for you, based on whom you call the most often. You can also nominate one of your Friends and Family numbers as your 'best friend', and get a 20% discount on calls to this number.

*Call Return* – This service allows you to find the number of the last person who called you, whether you answered the phone or not. You dial 1471 and a recorded voice will tell you the number of the last person to call, and the time they rang. If you do not want your number to be made available in this way, you can dial 141 before any number you ring. Call Return is a free service and you do not have to register to use it.

It's worth noting that the services available to you depend partly on the BT calling plan you opt for, and these change regularly. A range of calling plans exist, from the Light User Scheme (LUS) which offers rebates for people who only use their phone occasionally, to the various BT Together calling plans, which offer varying packages of free and discount calls, text messages, and so on. Some services such as Friends and Family are not available to people on the Light User Scheme.

If your business really takes off, you may find it desirable to have a second phone line installed. BT runs regular special offers to encourage people to get a second line, and it is well worth contacting BT Customer Services on 150 (0800 800 150 from a non-BT phone) to see what deals may be available. Internet users can check on prices and services by visiting BT's website at www.bt.com.

Finally, it is worth noting that the information provided here has referred specifically to BT, but a growing number of alternative telephone providers now also offer their services to home users. People in many areas have the option of using a cable company for their phone, and this can provide a cost-effective solution, particularly if you want the company's home entertainment package as well. Other phone companies use BT lines, but with different tariffs which again may be more attractive than

BT's. Against this, it should be noted that not all of the extra features listed above may be available to people using a telephone provider other than BT.

## Answering Machines

A telephone answering machine (TAM) is a particular asset for one-person businesses, as it means that if you are away from the phone the machine will take messages for you and perhaps prevent a lost customer. A wide range of machines is available from suppliers such as BT, electrical stores (e.g. Comet) and specialist phone shops. Prices start at around £20 and go up to £200 or more. Even the more basic machines have a range of extra features these days, including automatic dial-back, call forwarding, remote playback of messages, and recording the date and time of incoming calls.

Answering machines do have some disadvantages. For one thing, some people dislike them and will refuse to leave a message. Another is that a person hearing an answering machine on the other end of the line will get a clear impression that you are a small – probably one-person – enterprise. An alternative to the machine would be to engage an answering service to take calls on your behalf. Such services ensure that the phone is always answered by a human being, and they will take messages and pass them on to you. To identify such services in your area, look under 'Telephone Answering Services' in Yellow Pages.

## Mobile Phones

If your business involves working on your customers' premises – e.g. gardening or painting and decorating – you will almost certainly need a mobile phone to take customer enquiries. Even if you are only out some of the day, rather than use an answering machine you might prefer to have a mobile with you, and perhaps use BT's Call Diversion service to forward calls to this.

Mobile phones use radio rather than fixed lines, so they will operate almost anywhere. There are four well-established mobile phone operators in Britain – Vodafone, O2, Orange and T-Mobile – along with their newer rivals Hutchison 3G (trading as Three), Virgin and BT Mobile. The latter two companies do not have their own networks but use those of other companies.

Each company offers a range of different tariffs. These vary widely, some being more cost-effective for low users, others for those who make more frequent use. If you are considering obtaining a mobile phone for business purposes, research all the options carefully, and choose the network and tariff most appropriate to your needs. As well as the cost of the mobile itself (often very low in the UK), there is likely to be a monthly line rental and a charge for every call you make (though some free minutes and text messages are usually included in the rental). However, a growing range of pay-as-you-go tariffs is also available, and may be more cost-effective for home-based business use.

Although costs have come down considerably in recent years, mobile phones still tend to be more expensive than landlines, and it is important to check that the benefits to your business will justify the costs involved. Before making any purchase, therefore, obtain at least the current issue of a consumer periodical such as What Mobile? to check their recommendations. Some retailers such as Carphone Warehouse claim to offer unbiased advice on which mobile phone company and tariff would suit you best, based on your circumstances and anticipated pattern of usage. The quality of advice can vary, however, and it is best to speak to two or three potential suppliers before signing any contract.

Finally, a growing number of people are electing to cancel their landline phones altogether and use their mobile for all calls. This has the advantage that you save the paying the monthly rental on a landline that you may not use very often. Before you go down this path there are a few points to consider, however.

- Some older people in particular may be wary of calling a mobile phone number because they expect it will be expensive. You could lose a few potential customers who are put off by this.

- Mobile phones are more easily lost, stolen or damaged. If this happens to you and people are unable to contact you, it could prove expensive for your business.

- And finally, as mentioned above, call charges from mobiles still tend to be higher than from landline phones. You will need to consider carefully whether the savings from not paying rental for a landline phone will outweigh this.

## Fax Machines

*Fax machines* – more properly called facsimile machines – provide a means for transmitting written documents over telephone lines at the same price as an ordinary phone call. They can also be used – at a pinch – as basic photocopiers.

If you wish to obtain a fax machine, you will of course need a phone line to connect it to. If you want the fax to be switched on all the time, you will need a separate line and phone number for it. Some modern fax machines, however, can automatically determine whether an incoming call is a fax or voice call, and will route the call accordingly; thus you will need one line only. Fax machines can either be rented or bought.

Another alternative, if you have a computer with a modem (a device for connecting your computer with others via a phone line), is to use this for sending and receiving faxes. Most modern computers come pre-installed with software which will enable you to send, say, a word processed document to a fax machine. Many will also enable you to receive faxes, though this facility can be more awkward to set up and use.

Another alternative, and one that is growing in popularity, is to use an Internet-based faxing service such as eFax (www.efax.com). This and similar services provide you with a special phone number for incoming faxes. The faxes are then converted into emails and forwarded to your email address. The fax typically arrives as an image attached to the email; you can view this on your computer and, if you wish, print it out. These services also allow you to send faxes via the Internet. This is further discussed in the next section, Computers and the Internet.

# chapter 14

## Computers and the Internet

Many home-based businesses will benefit from having a computer, and for some types of business (e.g. desktop publishing, website design) they are indispensable. Home computers can help with a huge range of tasks, from preparing invoices to keeping accounts. They also give you the means to access the vast resources of the Internet (of which more later). Here are some of the main areas in which having a computer can be useful for home-based businesses.

## Word Processing

A word processing program makes a computer work like an electric typewriter, but with many additional features. Most importantly, when you are writing a letter or other document, the words are not immediately printed on paper as would be the case with a typewriter, but instead appear on a monitor screen. You can then edit your document – correcting mistakes, removing and adding text, and moving text around – until the letter is exactly how you want it. Only then do you need to print it out. With the help of a word processor, even inexperienced typists can produce highly professional-looking letters and documents.

Another big advantage of word processing is that documents can be stored electronically for re-use in future. This is a particular benefit when there are certain documents you send out regularly with only slight variations, e.g. invoices, statements and quotations. You can store such documents in the computer, then simply make any necessary amendments to things such as name, address, date and amount before printing them out. Many word processors also include a 'mailmerge' facility, whereby you can combine a standard letter with a list of names and addresses to produce a series of letters, each individually addressed to a person on your list.

Word processors also include a range of other facilities to help make writing quicker and easier and documents more professional-looking. Most include a spellchecker, which will identify any spelling mistakes in your document and substitute the correct version. Other facilities include automatic page numbering, bold text and italics, underlining, changing the size and style of text, and many more. The most popular word processing program today is Microsoft Word.

## Desktop Publishing

Desktop publishing (DTP) is similar to word processing, but the term tends to be used to describe the production of more elaborate documents such as newsletters, magazines and brochures. As well as text, such documents may include a wide range of visual elements, including diagrams, illustrations, graphs, photos, and so on. They are frequently set out in multiple columns, and use full-colour artwork. Modern word processors have a good range of desktop publishing facilities, though serious professionals use dedicated DTP programs such as Quark XPress.

The latter are not as good at manipulating text as straightforward word processing programs, so most also include the facility to import text created on a word processor.

Desktop publishing programs – and modern word processors – can enable you to produce high quality artwork for publicity materials and the like without the need to employ a graphic artist or designer. The programs do take some time (and possibly training) to master, and to use them well you really need some knowledge of design principles. But if you are prepared to put the time and effort in, even non-expert designers can produce highly professional looking documents.

## Spreadsheets

Spreadsheet programs enable you to store and manipulate numerical information. They are therefore ideal for purposes such as accounts and cashflow forecasts. Once your spreadsheet has been set up, you can simply enter the appropriate figures into it and it will automatically perform routine tasks such as adding up columns of figures for you.

Spreadsheet programs can also be used to calculate and print out invoices and quotations. For example, if you need to charge a client for twelve hours of work at £20.00 per hour plus expenses, a spreadsheet program can be set up to perform this calculation automatically for you and print out the appropriate invoice. Finally, most spreadsheet programs have the facility to convert the information contained within them into charts, graphs and diagrams. Putting information such as sales and advertising expenditure into this format can be very helpful when looking for underlying trends.

The best-known spreadsheet program today is Microsoft Excel.

## Databases

A database program is rather like a filing cabinet or card index, but because it is computerised it offers many advantages over manual systems. In a database program you can store the names, addresses and other details of customers and potential customers, suppliers, business contacts and so on. The computer allows you not only to keep and easily update these details, but to print them out on labels, envelopes, invoices, mailshots and so on. Database programs make it easy to find any record you want, for example by typing a single keyword such as the person's surname.

Database programs will also enable you to sort records, and select only those which meet certain criteria. For instance, you could, at the touch of a few keys, get a list of all your customers over the age of 25 (assuming age is in the information you keep), or all of those in a particular town or village. Databases are a particularly valuable tool in sales and marketing. For example, you could keep a database of all your customers, recording such details as when they last ordered, what they ordered, and how much. You could then get a list of all those customers who have NOT ordered from you in the last six months, and write them a letter reminding them about your services. Note, incidentally, that if you keep a database of your customers, you will almost certainly need to register with the Data Protection Registrar (see Appendix: Useful Organisations).

The one main drawback to database programs is that all the information has to be keyed in in the first place, and then kept up to date. Where there are large numbers of records, and large amounts of information stored on each, this can become a tedious and time-consuming exercise. In the end it is up to you to decide what information will be most useful to your business, and avoid putting irrelevant information onto the database just for the sake of it.

The most widely used database program is Microsoft Access.

## Presentation Graphics

Presentation graphics programs let you produce series of slides for business presentations. They allow you to combine words with images, animations and (if you want) sound effects too. Finished presentations are normally stored on a laptop computer and projected on a screen. Presentations to small numbers of people can also be done on a computer, or the pages of the presentation can simply be printed out.

Presentation graphics programs are only likely to be relevant if you have to give presentations when you are tendering for work (e.g. if you run a home-based advertising agency). They might also be of use if you are ever asked to give talks about your work. For example, a freelance writer might be asked to give a presentation at a writers' conference. In such cases, a presentation graphics program may be very useful or even a necessity.

The best known presentation graphics program is Microsoft Powerpoint.

## What Computer Should You Buy?

There is a vast range of computers, with new models appearing every day as manufacturers try to outdo one another with regard to price and performance. Especially if you are new to computing, it is important not just to buy the first machine you see, but to take some time to assess what you want and what is available. A huge range of magazines about computers is published today, and it is worth getting hold of some of those aimed at non-expert readers to try to get a feel for the market. A personal recommendation is Computer Active, an inexpensive, yet informative, weekly publication aimed primarily at home-based users.

If you have decided to buy a computer for your business, you will have a number of choices to make. The first is fairly straightforward – Macintosh or Windows. Almost all personal computers sold today use one or other of these operating systems. The great majority sold through the shops use Microsoft Windows, and most home-based business owners may prefer to obtain such a machine, if only because of the wider range of programs available to run on them. Windows computers also tend to be a bit cheaper. The main rival system is Macintosh. Macintosh computers are particularly strong on desktop publishing, video and music editing. If you intend to do any of these things on a regular basis, buying a 'Mac' may be an option you will want to consider.

Your second choice is whether to go for a laptop or a desktop computer. Laptops are all-in-one machines that can easily be carried around – so if you will want to use your computer in a variety of locations, one of these may be your best choice. Otherwise, desktop computers do have some advantages, though. You get more computing power for your money, and they can also be more comfortable to use. It's a personal choice, but if you don't need the portability of a laptop, a desktop computer may well be a better overall investment.

As well as the actual computer, you will also need to purchase a printer. There are two main types, each with their advantages and disadvantages.

Inkjet – These machines work by spraying tiny blobs of ink on to the page. Modern inkjet printers give good quality results, and are likely to be the only realistic choice if you want to print in colour. Their drawbacks are: (a) the relatively high running costs; (b) the fact that they need special, coated paper to give the best finish; and (c) the ink tends to spread, meaning that text does not always print as crisply as one would like. Note, also, that most inkjet ink is water-based, meaning that these printers are not suitable for printing labels and envelopes (they will smear in the rain!).

Laser – Laser printers give the highest quality output. A laser beam in the machine draws the characters in your document onto a drum. The drum attracts ink powder (toner) to the characters, and they are then transferred to paper. Laser printers tend to be more expensive than inkjets, but nowadays some excellent low cost black-and-white models are available. Laser-printed documents look crisp and professional, and the running costs are generally much lower. They also tend to be the fastest printers, especially for long documents.

## Buying Your Computer

Buying a computer for your business can be a daunting prospect. To avoid expensive mistakes, follow the checklist below.

(1) Decide exactly what you want your new computer to do for you. Will it be used mainly for word processing, or do you intend to use spreadsheets, databases, presentation graphics programs, and so on? Even if you only intend to use the computer for one or two applications initially, bear in mind that you may wish to add others later on.

(2) Speak to a number of possible suppliers, and explain exactly what you want your computer system to be able to do.

(3) Avoid getting sidetracked into detailed discussions about technical specifications – ensure that the supplier sticks to discussing what the computer will do for you.

(4) Ask to see the complete system working. Get the supplier to demonstrate the features that you yourself wish to use.

(5) Buy proven products that have been used successfully by others, not new and untested ones.

(6) Wherever possible buy an existing software package rather than having one designed for you from scratch. The latter procedure can be time-consuming and expensive.

(7) Be prepared to spend a little bit extra to get a system that will meet your needs now and in the foreseeable future. If you buy the cheapest system now, you may find yourself having to buy a new, more powerful system within a few months. As well as the inconvenience, this can work out more expensive than buying the more powerful system straight away.

(8) Particularly if you are new to computing, see whether the supplier will install the computer for you and take you through the initial steps of starting it up and using it. A growing range of suppliers offer this service, though the cost will be incorporated in the price you pay.

(9) Find out what after-sales support is available. Is there a period during which, if the computer breaks down, the supplier will replace it or repair it free of charge? In this case, will you have to take the computer back to the supplier, or will they come to your premises? Is there a telephone number you can ring for advice and support? Ensure that any guarantees made by the supplier are put in writing.

(10) And finally, never rush in to buying a computer. Before you sign on the dotted line, think carefully about what you need and whether the system you are buying will meet those needs. If possible, get a second opinion from a friend, colleague or relative who has some knowledge of computers.

## The Internet

As mentioned earlier, one big advantage of having a computer is that it enables you to access the resources of the Internet. I assume that some readers of this book will be regular net users already, but others may have little if any experience in this field. So let's start with the basics...

The Internet is a world-wide network of inter-connected computers. It began in the USA and is still American dominated, but it is not under the control of any particular government or agency. Anyone with a suitable computer can log in via an Internet access provider (IAP) and gain access to information stored on millions of computers across the world. Not only that, you can advertise your business with your very own Internet 'homepage', and communicate with other computer users world-wide free of charge by e-mail.

The Internet actually consists of a number of different networks and services. By far the best known is the World Wide Web (web for short); this is the most technically sophisticated area of the Internet. Viewers explore web sites using a browser program, and can move quickly and easily from one site to another via so-called hyperlinks (a process popularly known as surfing the web). Other services that may be of interest to home-based business owners include newsgroups, Internet telephony, and – of course – e-mail.

## How Do You Join Up?

At the risk of stating the obvious, the first thing you will need is a computer. The good news is that most home computers sold today are set up to make connecting to the Internet as easy as possible.

Until recently, many people accessed the net using dial-up. This involved connecting your computer to an ordinary phone line using a device called a modem. When you wanted to use the Internet, your computer automatically dialled a special number provided by your IAP. Once the connection was made, you could then browse the web, check your e-mails, and so on.

Dial-up services are still available, but they are slow and tie up your home phone line. Unless you really don't intend using the Internet more than once in a blue moon (and you almost certainly will use it more than this once you see its potential) you really should consider signing up for a 'broadband' service.

Broadband Internet services are much faster than dial-up. A broadband connection will let you make the most of what the Internet has to offer. In addition, broadband services are 'always on', and will not tie up your phone line for voice calls. You can get broadband via your existing telephone line from suppliers such as BT, or from cable providers such as Virgin Media if cable is laid in your area. People in more remote locations can also use other methods such as satellite broadband, but these tend to cost more.

At one time broadband Internet was much more expensive than dial-up, but with the fierce competition among broadband providers, this is no longer the case. Basic broadband access is now available for as little as £10 a month. For very fast broadband access you will have to pay more, but for the typical home-business user this will not be necessary (very fast broadband is only likely to be needed if you intend regularly to download movies and other large files, or to play certain interactive online games).

This is not the place for a lengthy discussion of the pros and cons of different IAPs; newsstand magazines such as Web User and .Net publish all the detailed, up-to-date information you could possibly need. It is, however, well worth speaking to friends and colleagues who are already connected to the net at home, and asking about their experiences and recommendations.

## What Can You Do on the Internet?

As mentioned earlier, there are several Internet services that are likely to be of interest to people running home-based businesses. These include e-mail, newsgroups, Internet telephony and the World Wide Web. Let's look at each of these in turn.

### 1. E- Mail

E-mail is, of course, short for 'electronic mail'. It provides a simple method of exchanging messages with other Internet users, be they on the next street or the other side of the world. The main benefits of this are (a) the low cost, and (b) the speed of delivery (compared with conventional mail services). You don't have to be connected all the time in order to receive your incoming mail. All IAPs offer a mailbox facility, whereby messages sent to your e-mail address are stored till you next log on to collect them.

When you sign up with an IAP, the provider will give you an e-mail address (some offer more than one, so that colleagues, or other members of your family, can have their own e-mail addresses as well). Once you have written your e-mail, you can send it to anyone you wish as long as you know their e-mail address. A typical e-mail address would be: jane.smith@aol.com. There is no cost involved in sending e-mails (other than the monthly fee to your IAP, which you pay anyway).

For home-based business owners, e-mail offers several potential attractions. Principally, you can correspond quickly and cheaply with clients and potential clients across the UK, and even in other countries. And, once you have an e-mail address, clients will have a quick, cheap and simple way of getting in touch with you; the advantages of this will be obvious. You may be able to submit invoices and other correspondence by e-mail, thus saving on postage and stationery. And in certain types of business (e.g. freelance writing and indexing), you may actually be able to submit your work via e-mail, again saving time and money.

## 2. Newsgroups

These are, if you like, the next step up after e-mail. A newsgroup is basically an electronic noticeboard devoted to a particular subject. Anyone accessing a newsgroup can read messages other people have sent in and, if they wish, reply or 'post' a message of their own.

There are many thousands of newsgroups devoted to any subject you can imagine (and quite a few you probably can't). They are divided into families each of which shares a common prefix such as rec (for recreation) or misc (miscellaneous). Examples include rec.arts.film and misc.writing.

Newsgroups are full of enthusiasts who like nothing better than to talk about their pet subject. They might not appeal to everyone as a way of passing the time, but they can sometimes be very useful for business owners as a means of solving problems. For example, a mobile mechanic needing to find a spare part for a vintage sports car might post a request in the newsgroup uk.rec.cars.classic, with a very good chance that someone reading his message would respond with the information he required.

## 3. Internet telephony

It is also possible to phone people via the Internet using online services such as Skype (www.skype.com). Two Skype users can talk free of charge over the net for as long as they like, even if they are on different sides of the world.

Even if the person you wish to speak to is not on Skype, using the so-called Skype-Out service you can phone them from your computer and only the last leg of the call will be routed over conventional phone lines.

The result is that you can phone people in other countries at much lower rates than normal.

To use Internet telephony services, you will need a special headset, or alternatively a dedicated Internet phone that you plug in to your computer. Once you have this in place, however, making Internet phone calls is almost as simple as using an ordinary phone, and the quality is generally as good. It is, however, worth noting that to use Internet telephony successfully, you will almost certainly need a broadband connection.

### 4. The World Wide Web

The World Wide Web (often shortened to the web) is the largest and fastest growing part of the internet. It is also the part that receives by far the greatest publicity. Indeed, new users could be forgiven for thinking that the web IS the Internet!

There are literally millions of documents on the web. Some are businesses advertising their wares, while others are run by universities, government institutions, and so on. Quite a few are run by clubs and societies and, of course, by private individuals.

As well as text, web pages can contain photos, sound and video clips, animations, and so on. In addition, web pages have one other very important feature – the so-called hyperlinks. These are short cuts to other documents on the web. By clicking on a hyperlink you can be transported instantly to another web page, even if it is hosted on a computer the other side of the world. This makes the web a very powerful tool for research.

Every page on the web has a unique URL (uniform resource locator). Once you know the URL of a site, you have all the information you need to visit it. For example, the URL of the Friends of the Earth site is www.foe.co.uk. To access websites, as mentioned above, you will need to use a program called a browser. All new computers come with a browser pre-installed. On Windows machines this is Microsoft Internet Explorer, but there are others (e.g. Firefox) you can download via the net if you prefer.

The web is an invaluable source of information on any subject imaginable, but finding the information you want from the mass of documents it contains can be tricky. Indeed, one writer says, 'The Internet is like an enormous library in which someone has turned out the lights and tipped the index cards all over the floor.'

Fortunately it's not completely needle-in-a-haystack, however. Help is at hand in the form of search engines. As the name suggests, these are programs that will help you find documents on the web relevant to the subject you are interested in. They all work slightly differently, but typically you enter a key word or phrase, and the search engine then checks its records and comes up with a list of sites in which your word (or words) can be found. You can then go directly to these sites via the hyperlinks provided. The most popular search engine by some distance today is Google at www.google.com.

Search engines are powerful tools, and again they are free to use. They can be used for a wide range of purposes, including identifying suppliers and potential customers, researching the latest developments in your field, and finding online stores selling books and other products (frequently at lower prices than those you will pay in the high street).

*Setting up your own web homepage*

One other big attraction of the World Wide Web is that you can use it to advertise your business by creating your own 'homepage'. Various firms will do this for you – for a price – but it is actually not difficult to create a basic homepage of your own. Most IAPs provide space on the web as part of their service package. They will also usually provide the basic software (tools) to create a homepage suitable for publishing on the web. As a general principle, it is important that your business homepage should be attractive, informative and (if possible) entertaining. People who are surfing the web have a huge range of sites they can visit – and if yours does not immediately grab their interest, they will swiftly move on somewhere else.

# chapter 15

## Tax, National Insurance and VAT

As Benjamin Franklin famously observed, there are only two things any of us can be sure of in this life: death and taxes. As a self-employed business person, it will be your responsibility to keep records of your business income and expenditure so that you can declare them to the authorities, and in due course pay tax on them.

Book-keeping is discussed a little later on in the book. It is, however, worth emphasising that, while all business income must be declared for tax purposes, you can set against this any expenditure directly related to your business. This will include obvious things like the cost of raw materials, stationery, postage, printing and photocopying, business bank charges, a proportion of your home phone bills, and so on. In addition, you should be able to deduct the costs of any journeys related to your work, including visits to clients, printers, your bank, etc. Should you decide to join a relevant trade or professional organisation, you can claim their membership fee. You can also set against income the cost of any business-related training you undertake and business publications you subscribe to. Finally, if you are working from home, you can claim a proportion of your household bills (gas, electricity, water, etc.) against tax. If you are a home-owner, however, this may have implications for your liability to capital gains tax when you sell your house, so it would be advisable to speak to an accountant about this first.

## Income Tax

The amount of income tax you have to pay depends on a range of factors. As you will probably know, everyone in the UK has a tax-free personal allowance. For the tax year 2008/09, the basic personal allowance was £5,435. Once your earnings in a year exceed this, you start to pay tax at whatever may be the going rate. For the tax year 2008/09, tax was due at 20 per cent on taxable earnings of up to £34,800. Any income above this was taxed at a rate of 40 per cent.

Note that the figures above are based on your income from all sources. If you have another full-time or part-time job, this may well use up your tax-free allowance, and in that case you will pay tax at the appropriate rate on all your business earnings.

Self-employed people declare their income to HM Revenue & Customs (HMRC), and pay tax by two instalments in January and July each year (unless the amount owed is very small, in which case it may be collected in one instalment or by an adjustment to your personal allowance for the following year).

If your business is set up as a limited company different rules apply, and you will need to take advice from an accountant. You are most likely to be paid in the form of a salary from the company, on which you will have to pay tax monthly like any employee, and dividends, which for tax purposes are treated differently again. Your accountant will advice you on the most tax-efficient combination of payment methods for your particular circumstances.

As soon as you start earning money from your home-based business, you should notify HMRC; they will then send you the necessary forms to fill in. The office to contact will be the one covering the area where you live (assuming you are working from home). This may well be different from your former PAYE tax office, which will have been based on your employer's address, not yours.

Up-to-date information about tax rates, allowances and so on is available from the HMRC website at www.hmrc.gov.uk.

## National Insurance

The National Insurance Contributions Office (formally part of the Department of Social Security, now a division of HMRC) must also be informed of your business activities for National Insurance purposes. The position is somewhat complex, but the main points are summarised here. An employee taxed under the PAYE (pay as you earn) system normally pays a fixed proportion of his or her earnings (currently 11%) in National Insurance contributions. This is deducted directly by the employer, who also makes a further contribution himself.

A self-employed person, by contrast, pays his/her National Insurance in two parts. Class 2 contributions are fixed payments made every week, normally by direct debit. For 2008/09, the weekly rate for self-employed people was £2.30. If you believe your earnings from self-employment are likely to be low, you can apply for exemption from paying Class 2 National Insurance. The low earnings limit for the 2008/09 tax year was £4,825. If you wish to apply for exemption, you can do so on HMRC leaflet CF10 'Self-employed people with small earnings'. This is available from local tax offices or direct from the National Insurance Contributions Office (address below). It is, however, worth noting that if you do not pay Class 2 contributions, it may affect your pension rights and your entitlement to some social security benefits.

Class 4 contributions are an additional levy made on earnings within certain limits. Unlike Class 2 contributions, they do not provide any entitlement to social security benefits, and are really just another form of taxation. They are assessed and collected by HMRC along with Income Tax. In the year 2008/09, Class 4 contributions were payable by self-employed people at a rate of 8% on earnings between £5,435 and £40,040. On any earnings above the upper limit you still pay Class 4 contributions, but at a lower rate of just 1%.

For any enquiries about National Insurance, or to provide notification that you are setting up in business, write to: HMRC, National Insurance Contributions Office, Benton Park View, Newcastle-upon-Tyne, NE98 1ZZ, tel. 0845 302 1479. Information is also available via the website www.hmrc.gov.uk/nic.

## Value Added Tax (VAT)

If your taxable turnover (as opposed to net profit) exceeds a set figure at the end of any twelve-month period, you are obliged to register for VAT. Once registered, you will then have to charge VAT at the current rate to your clients, and pass this on to the local VAT office (a division of HMRC) at regular intervals. Because of the relatively high VAT threshold in the UK (currently £64,000 and raised most years), the majority of people running home-based businesses are unlikely to have to register when starting out.

Many small businesses attempt to postpone VAT registration as long as possible because of the extra paperwork it entails. Registration can have some advantages, however. Although you have to collect VAT from your clients, once you are registered you can also reclaim the VAT you pay on business supplies (materials, stationery, training, petrol, etc.). In addition, being registered for VAT can give your business added credibility among clients and suppliers.

It is possible to register for VAT voluntarily even if your turnover is below the threshold. You might want to do this if you believe that the advantages to your business will justify the extra paperwork involved. To do this, you will need to satisfy HMRC that your activities constitute a proper 'business for VAT purposes'. Bear in mind, also, that if you take this course you will have to add VAT to all your customers' bills (unless your particular line of business is zero-rated, e.g. selling books or young children's clothing). If customers cannot reclaim this themselves, it may make your service or products less attractive to them.

If you would like more information about VAT registration at any stage, you should ask for HMRC Notice 700/1 'Should I be registered for VAT?' from your local tax office. Information is also available on the HMRC website at www.hmrc.gov.uk.

# chapter 16

## Pricing your services

For many people running small businesses, putting a price on their products and services is one of the hardest tasks they have to perform. Setting prices is something of a balancing act. If you set your prices too low you may fail to cover all your costs and end up losing money rather than making it. Clearly no business can survive long in those circumstances! On the other hand, if you set your prices too high, people may be unwilling to buy from you, especially if they can buy the same product or service more cheaply from one of your competitors.

It follows from this that in setting prices both the cost of providing the product or service, and the price that the customer will be willing to pay, must be taken into account. In different types of business, however, this applies in different ways.

## Pricing a Product

If your business will involve producing a product (e.g. toys or craft items), the price you charge will have to cover the cost of the raw materials plus your overheads (heating, lighting, advertising, stationery and so on) and also give you a reasonable profit. The simplest way to price each unit is therefore as follows:

Selling price = cost of materials per unit + $\dfrac{\text{total overheads}}{\text{total production}}$ + mark-up

The total overheads includes, for this purpose, the cost of labour, whether it is yours or (later on) that of your employees. The selling price therefore covers all your fixed and variable costs, while the mark-up is what will give your business its profit. This may be best explained by an example.

## EXAMPLE

Nita plans to set up a home-based business making soft toys. She intends to buy the materials and kapok (stuffing) and assemble the toys herself. Nita estimates that she can make one soft toy per hour, with raw materials costing £2 per toy. Working forty hours a week, she can therefore produce 40 toys every week. She must now work out what she should charge for her labour per hour.

One simple approach to this problem is to charge what you would have to pay an employee to do the job. After all, if the business really takes off and Nita has to take on someone to help her, she will need to pay this person the 'going rate' for the job. If this rate is much more than she has been paying herself, she will either have to raise her prices or lower her profits, neither of which is likely to be an attractive option. By studying job advertisements in her local paper, Nita estimates that the usual rate for this type of job is around £240 for a 40-hour week. To work out an hourly rate, she adds another 50% to this, to take into account such things as paid holidays and sick leave, extra taxes, and the higher overheads taking on an employee would entail. So, in Nita's case, the hourly rate comes to (£240 + 50%)/40 = £9.00 an hour.

Nita must now work out her total fixed costs (overheads) per year. By paying herself £9.00 per hour and working 49 forty-hour weeks (leaving three weeks for holidays), Nita's annual 'wages' come out as 9.00 x 49 x 40 = £17,640. Nita estimates that her other overheads will be around £3,000 every year, giving her a total overheads figure of £20,640. Nita's yearly production will be 40 x 49 = 1960 toys, and she decides to aim for a mark-up of 30%. The pricing calculation therefore comes out as follows:

$$\text{Selling price per toy} = £2 + \frac{17,640}{1,960} + 30\% = £14.30$$

Having worked out a selling price, Nita must now check whether people will be prepared to pay such a sum for one of her toys. She hopes to sell most of her production through shops. As a rule-of-thumb, non-food products sell at about double the retailer's cost price, so a likely retail price for one of Nita's soft toys would be around £29.00. Retailers will soon tell Nita whether her toys will sell at that price. If not, Nita will have to reduce her prices, either by cutting the cost of raw materials (though potential savings here are limited), increasing her productivity (i.e. producing toys at a faster rate than one per hour), cutting her rate of pay (though this in unlikely to be an attractive option) or changing the design.

---

One point arising from this is that Nita is paying herself a wage but also making a profit from her mark-up. Perhaps it may seem as though Nita is paying herself twice, and you might wonder why she does not simply pay herself a wage and have done. However, if all Nita makes from her business is the £9.00 an hour she pays herself, she might as well be doing a paid job for someone else and letting them worry about marketing, book-keeping, pricing and so on! The profit is extra income which recompenses Nita for the risks and extra work entailed in running a business, and that is why you should normally budget to make one. Nita may decide to take all of her profits herself – in which case she will be taxed on it as income – or she may choose to re-invest some or all of it in new equipment such as an electric sewing machine which may improve her productivity.

One other point is that Nita's calculations assumed she would be working the whole time just on making toys. In practice this is unlikely, as any business owner also has to spend time on many tasks which do not make any direct contribution to profit. These may include:

- book-keeping
- seeing customers and potential customers
- getting money from customers when it is overdue
- buying materials and finding better sources of supply
- preparing advertisements, leaflets, letters, price lists, etc.
- planning and organising future work
- maintaining and repairing equipment
- dealing with officials
- travelling
- dealing with correspondence, etc.

In deciding what to charge, remember that you will need time for all of these things and more, in addition to the time you can devote to productive, profit-making work. If you are a sole trader, you are likely to find at least 25% of your time will be spent on these other matters.

## Pricing a Service

Many home-based businesses, instead of making products, involve providing a service. In service-based businesses pricing is normally based on an hourly rate for the job, plus the cost of materials.

If you are running a service business then, rather than a product, what you are really selling is your time. Putting a price on this is therefore crucial. One possible approach is to decide on your target annual income, then work out the number of hours you will be able to charge to customers during the year. By dividing your target income by the number of chargeable hours, you will come up with the amount you need to charge per hour to achieve your target income.

Bear in mind, however, that you will not be able to spend every hour of the day on chargeable work. Some time, inevitably, will have to be spent on tasks such as book-keeping, marketing, administration, and so on. Typically, in a service business around 20 to 40 percent of your time may have to be spent on tasks that are not immediately chargeable to a customer.

As with a manufacturing business, you will need to include in your hourly rate an amount to cover your overheads and an amount to provide a profit. The total hourly rate you charge will be according to the following formula:

$$\text{Hourly rate} = \frac{\text{Target annual income} + \text{total overheads} + \text{target profits}}{\text{Total chargeable hours per year}}$$

This calculation will give you an hourly rate, but you need to check how it compares with other, similar businesses. This is where market research is so important. If your hourly rates are much higher than other businesses, you will have problems attracting customers, and need to look at ways of bringing your rate down. Possible options would include working longer hours, or reducing your target income, overheads or profit margin.

## EXAMPLE

Mark plans to start his own building business. He decides that he will work 49 weeks a year, and will aim for an average of 30 hours a week chargeable work. This gives him 1,470 chargeable hours per year. His target income for the first year is £12,000. The hourly rate he will need to earn to achieve this therefore comes out as:

$$\frac{12,000}{1,470} = \text{£8.16 per hour}$$

The actual rate Mark charges his customers, however, needs to include in addition an element to cover his overheads and an element for profit. Mark estimates that his annual fixed costs (excluding what he pays himself) will come to £4,000 and he will aim for £2,000 profit in his first year. Mark's total hourly rate which he must charge customers to meet all these requirements is therefore:

$$\frac{12,000 + 4,000 + 2,000}{1470} = \text{£12.24 per hour}$$

*Charging for Materials*

As well as your hourly rate, the fees you charge clients will also need to cover the materials you use and any other variable costs. (An example of another variable cost would be the cost of subcontracting part of a job – that is, paying someone else to do it instead of doing it yourself.)

One common way of charging for materials is 'at cost'. However, this need not necessarily mean that you charge the customer the same amount as you paid for them. To do so would be to ignore the hidden costs of such things as the time you take to find and buy materials, the cost of keeping them in stock, the cost of travelling to pick them up, and so on. Some businesses define 'at cost' as the retail price which a private customer would pay, whereas they themselves purchase at trade or wholesale prices. This difference helps recompense their other costs. Depending on your business, this may well be a sensible policy.

## The Perils of Under-charging

Before leaving this topic, it is worth making the point that many people when starting out in business make the mistake of under-charging. Their reasons include:

- They forget the need to cover all their overheads and make a reasonable profit.
- They believe they lack the experience or skills to command higher rates.
- They think they will have to charge less than existing businesses to win customers away from them.
- Or they simply take the view that any work (and income) is better than none.

In the short term under-charging may well attract customers. However, it is very likely that the income generated will be insufficient to cover all your costs and still leave you with enough income to live on. Furthermore, once your customers have become accustomed to paying 'bargain basement' fees, you are likely to face stiff resistance from them if you try to raise charges later. And finally, many people (rightly or wrongly) associate low fees with shoddy workmanship. Clients whose first priority is a good-quality job may therefore actually be put off if the prices you quote appear suspiciously low.

For the long-term success of your business it is much better to work out target rates of payment according to the principles set out above and use these as your basis for charging. Of course, sometimes a potential client may respond that the fee quoted is higher than he or she expected. In this case, you may have to decide how much you want (or need) their custom. If you have no other work on and the amount charged will still cover your costs and produce some sort of profit, you may decide to accept a lower fee. However, you should be aware that the client who wants the lowest price is often the one who will be the most demanding of your time and the most critical of your service.

Pricing is an essential aspect of operating a successful business. Concern yourself with what the competition is charging by all means, but ensure that you cover all your costs, including time and expenses, plus a reasonable profit margin. Once you have established your reputation, you can then raise your prices.

# chapter 17

## Marketing and selling

This is arguably the most important aspect of running any business, large or small. Marketing involves identifying who your potential customers will be (through market research) and tailoring your product/service to meet their needs. It also involves bringing your business to these people's attention and persuading them to buy.

Marketing covers not only advertising and selling, but a host of other factors that can affect your success or failure in attracting work. These include the prices you charge, the range of products and services you offer, your location, public relations, sales promotions (e.g. special offers), and so on. This section will concentrate on advertising and selling – but it is important to bear in mind that these are just two of a number of marketing ingredients that you will need to be aware of and try to manipulate to your business's advantage.

## Advertising

Advertising aims to bring a product or service to the attention of potential customers, and persuade them – or start to persuade them – to buy. When spending money on advertising you hope to recover your costs and more – hopefully much more – from increased sales. Advertising is not a precise science, however, and results can never be guaranteed. In general, if you have enough customers coming to you by word-of-mouth recommendation, there is little point in advertising.

If you do decide to advertise, you should have some kind of plan or strategy to guide you. The aim of your advertising strategy should be to bring potential customers from a state of ignorance about your product or service to a desire to purchase it. Your advertising should:

- get customers' attention
- help them understand the product or service
- get them to believe in the benefits you are offering
- make them want to buy your product or service
- get them to take action (e.g. fill in a coupon or make a phone call)
- improve the business's image and reputation

No one advertisement on its own can be expected to achieve all this. Rather, you will need to use a mixture of different types of advertising over a period of time. The latter point is particularly important. It is easy to believe, if you have taken out a half-page advertisement in your local paper, that everybody in the area now knows about your business. This is a mistake. People forget about adverts almost as soon as they have read them, unless they happen to need your product or service at that particular moment. It is therefore very important, if you are going to use advertising, to advertise regularly.

Regular advertising has other benefits as well. For one thing, if an individual sees your advertisement every week or month, your name is more likely to come into his mind should he at some point have need of your services. For another, if you advertise regularly, people will, in general, be more inclined to see your business as established and reliable, and unlikely to disappear overnight with their money. This is one reason why you will sometimes see businesses advertising 'established 1995' (or whatever). It all helps give an impression of stability and reliability.

On the other hand, it must be said that in some types of business regular advertising may cause a degree of suspicion among potential customers. Tradesmen such as builders and plumbers, for example, tend to obtain much of their work through personal recommendation from satisfied customers. If such individuals advertise regularly, some people may conclude that if they need to advertise that much they cannot be very good! It is difficult to give hard-and-fast advice about this, as so much depends on local factors (e.g. are there many other businesses in the area offering this service, or just a few?). The best advice is to put yourself in the place of a potential customer. If you saw a business such as yours advertising every week, would you be impressed by this or suspicious about it?

## Where Can You Advertise?

When deciding where to advertise you have a wide range of media to choose from. Some, however, are more likely to be relevant than others. Large companies may use television, national newspapers, national commercial radio, and so on, but for a small business the cost of this is likely to be prohibitive. In addition, if your business serves just your local community, there is little point spending money sending your message to other parts of the country.

For many home-based businesses, the most fruitful forms of advertising are likely to include local newspapers, magazines and directories; brochures and leaflets; advertising cards; and mail shots. Let's look at each of these in turn.

*(1) Local newspapers, magazines and directories*

For many small businesses, these are likely to be among the first choice of places to advertise. Your aim should be to choose a publication seen by as many people as possible within your target area. For example, if you are aiming to provide a service to householders living within a 5 km radius of your business, you should choose a publication covering that area and preferably (to ensure that your advertising is as cost-effective as possible) no wider.

Having chosen the publication, or publications, you wish to advertise in, you must then decide on the size of your advertisement and what you want to say in it. Most newspapers and magazines offer both 'classified' and 'display' advertising. Classified advertisements – also known as lineage – normally consist of a few lines of text under a particular heading (e.g. builders, car repairs, electrical). They are usually charged at a price per word. Display advertisements – which can also include cartoons, graphics, and so on – are charged for by the amount of space they take up. Small display advertisements are charged per single column centimetre (scc), which is a space one column wide and one centimetre deep. Publications may also quote the cost per 1/8, 1/4, 1/2 or full page. There may be an extra charge if you want your advertisement in a particular position, e.g. on the front or back cover.

Classified advertisements are cheaper, and for many businesses can be a cost-effective way of attracting customers, especially if repeated regularly. They can also be a good way of 'testing' a new publication to see the level of interest an advert in it generates. Display advertisements are obviously more eye-catching than classified, but before going down this route you need to be confident that the extra response such an advertisement may generate will be sufficient to justify the extra expenditure.

What goes on your advertisement is up to you (or your agency, if you decide to employ one), but the guidelines below may be helpful.

- Have a clear, straightforward message.
- Use as few words as you can to get your message across.
- In display ads, try to come up with of a catchy headline that sums up the main benefit your business offers to its customers.
- Throughout the advertisement, go on emphasising the benefits of your product or service to the customer.
- Keep yourself in the background – talk about 'you' (the customer) rather than 'we' or 'I'.
- Avoid making extravagant claims and promises you cannot keep

(people will not believe you, and you may end up in trouble with the law).

- Avoid being funny – other people may not share your sense of humour.
- In a display advertisement, use pictures or photographs wherever possible.
- At the end of the advertisement, make it clear to readers what to do next ('Ring 070 9000 now for an instant quote', 'Return the coupon below for a free brochure'.)

It is also a good idea to study other people's advertisements, both your competitors' and other businesses'. If the same advert is repeated week after week, this is a good sign that it is having the desired effect of bringing in customers. See if you can work out what is making these advertisements successful, and try to apply what you have learned in your own advertising. Do not simply copy other people's advertisements, but it may be possible to adapt ideas, especially from businesses in other sectors, in your own advertising.

Finally, it is important to monitor the effectiveness of your advertising, so that you can see what works and what doesn't. Do not merely rely on personal impressions ('That advert looked good'), as these are often misleading. Keep a count of the actual number of replies you get to each advertisement, and also the number that translate into actual sales. If you are advertising in a number of places, you will need some means of separating out responses to each advertisement. One way of doing this is to include a 'keying device'. This is normally a code inserted in the address that tells you where people have got your details from. For example, if you have an advertisement in the Littletown News asking people to write to you for information, you could put 'Dept LN' after your business's name. Then, every time you get a letter with 'Dept LN' in the address, you will know that it came from that source. If people phone, you can of course just ask them where they saw your number.

## (2) Brochures and leaflets

Leaflets and brochures can carry more information than an advertisement, as more space is available to you. The message they convey is also intended to last a lot longer. As most people will not bother to cut out and keep an advertisement, a newspaper advertisement will last only as long as the newspaper it is contained in. After a few days, at most, it will therefore be thrown away. A well-designed and informative leaflet or brochure, by contrast, may be kept for future reference, perhaps for many months.

Brochures are small booklets. They normally consist of a few pages folded down the middle and stapled, perhaps with a card cover. Their most common uses are to send out to people enquiring about your services, perhaps in response to a newspaper advertisement. They may also be sent to existing customers or to people who have bought from you in the past. Brochures may include prices, or – to prevent them going out of date too soon – you may decide to insert a separate price list at the back. Brochures are a relatively cheap and cost-effective method of advertising, so long as they are distributed to people who have a genuine interest in purchasing from you.

Leaflets are even simpler than brochures. They consist of just one or two pages, or perhaps a single page folded over. Because they are so cheap to produce, leaflets can be more widely used than brochures. They can be given out at exhibitions, used in mailshots, inserted in newspapers and magazines (for which you will, of course, have to pay a fee), dropped through people's letterboxes, or even handed out to passers-by in the street.

Although leaflets and brochures are inexpensive, it is important that their appearance should not detract from the image you are trying to project. So they should not look too cheap and tatty, and the style should be consistent with your letterhead and packaging. As with advertisements, the main message in a leaflet or brochure should concern the benefits of your product or service to the customer. Keep the style relaxed and informal, almost as though you were writing a letter to a friend. Unless you are specifically aiming at technical people, avoid going into great technical detail. If such information is needed, it is normally better to keep the main text jargon-free and put product specifications, test data and so on in a separate section at the back.

When writing a leaflet or brochure, the same general principles apply as for writing advertisements, though you can and should go into more detail about your service. In addition, to achieve maximum effect the design must be good. Modern word processing and desktop publishing programs can produce professional-looking results using the templates they come supplied with, but if you do not have one of these (or are not confident about their use), it may be best to obtain professional help. Many high street printers will advise and assist in preparing artwork for a leaflet or brochure, or for a higher quality (but more expensive) service you could try a commercial artist or graphic designer. Advertising agents will also undertake this work, although their charges can be high. For many home-based businesses employing an agency, in the beginning at least, may not be viable or cost-effective.

*(3) Advertising cards*

Another option well worth considering is advertising cards. These are similar in size to business cards, around 10 x 6 centimetres being typical. Cards are very cheap to produce, and can be used in similar ways to leaflets. They are particularly useful when advertising businesses such as taxi services, which people may need at short notice. Advertising cards can be left in hotels, restaurants, cafes, bars, telephone booths, shops, nightclubs and so on, either in small piles on a table or stuck to the wall (though it may be best to obtain the proprietor's permission first!).

Cards can also be put through people's letterboxes. Because of their handy size, people may be more inclined to put them in a purse or wallet for future use than they would with a leaflet. One idea which some firms have adopted is to print their own message on one side of the card, and on the other include a list of phone numbers such as the local police, hospital, fire service, etc. The aim is to make the card more useful to the recipient, so there is more likelihood that he or she will keep it safe for future reference.

*(4) Mailshots*

A mailshot involves sending advertising material through the post to potential customers. This approach is also known as direct mail. The effectiveness of a mailshot depends on two things:

- The accuracy of the mailing list
- The impact of what you have written

For a successful mailshot, an accurate mailing list is essential. Writing to people who have gone away, gone out of business, died, or are not interested in your product or service is a waste of time and money. The best way of building up a mailing list is to start with people who have bought from you in the past, or at least enquired about your products or services. You can add to this by obtaining names from directories, trade associations and so on. If, for example, you are selling printing supplies, you may be able to obtain the names and addresses of all the printers in your area from a local directory.

You could also consider exchanging mailing lists with other non-competing businesses, buying or renting them. If you buy a list you can use it as often as you like, but lists are seldom sold outright. More often, you will have to rent a list, which means you are allowed to use it once only and cannot copy the names on it (though if any of the people you mail become your customers, you can then legitimately add them to your own mailing list). Specialist agents called list brokers can supply mailing lists in a wide range of categories, usually for rental. Lists available may include anything from single people to over-sixties, art collectors to vegetarians, business opportunity seekers to millionaires! Details of a range of list brokers can be obtained from the Direct Marketing Association (DMA), DMA House, 70 Margaret Street, London, W1W 8SS (Tel. 020 7291 3300). Information is also available from their website at www.dma.org.uk.

Mailshots should not be too long. One popular approach is to include a sales leaflet and a covering letter. In the letter you introduce yourself and explain what you are offering, emphasising – as ever – the benefits of your product or service to the customer. The accompanying leaflet should reinforce the sales message and leave recipients in no doubt as to what they should do next. If this is to write for further details, you could include a stamped and addressed envelope. If you want them to phone, ensure your number is printed prominently at the foot of the page.

Bear in mind that large mailshots can be costly. It is therefore essential that they are well-targeted at people who have a genuine interest in buying from you, or the profits may not cover the costs involved. For small, home-based businesses, the best approach may be to begin by writing to existing customers with special offers and so on. If this proves successful, you may try writing to other potential buyers as well; but be very cautious before spending large amounts. If you are using a new, untried mailing list, start with a small test mailing – one or two hundred letters perhaps – and only try a larger number if the response to the test mailing proves encouraging.

Royal Mail has a range of services such as Mailsort aimed at businesses who wish to use direct mail – see the section Help From Royal Mail for more details. It is also worth contacting the Direct Mail Information Service, who provide a range of free information and services (as well as some you have to pay for). Their address is Direct Mail Information Service, Mail Media Centre, Stukely Street, London, WC1V 7AB, tel. 020 7421 2250. See also their website at www.dmis.co.uk.

## Personal Selling

Advertising will begin the selling process but, for most products and services, completing the sale will require some degree of personal involvement, either face-to-face or over the phone. Selling is a skill that comes more readily to some people than to others, but there are certain principles you can learn which should help make it easier.

### (1) Face-to-face

This could occur in a variety of situations: a builder meeting a potential client, a toy-maker talking to a retailer, a private investigator talking to a solicitor, a writer or artist arranging a school visit, and so on. You may be 'cold calling', that is arriving unannounced, or you may be calling to fulfil an appointment made as a result of your advertising. Whatever the circumstances, making a good first impression is essential. Your skills (and self-confidence) are sure to improve with practice, but below are some guidelines that should get you off on the right track.

- Make sure that your appearance is smart and businesslike. Though it should hardly need saying, ensure that your grooming and personal hygiene are beyond reproach.

- Take adequate sales material – samples, business cards, brochures, order forms, and so on – and ensure that you know it thoroughly. Bring an up-to-date price list, and perhaps a pocket calculator in case you have to work out a price there and then. For some types of business – e.g. website design – a laptop computer may be essential.

- Prepare a written outline of your sales approach, so that you know what you are going to say when you meet a potential customer and the specific points you want to make. This is not to say you should have a script – it is important to listen carefully to what the customer tells you and respond accordingly – but you should have a general idea of the structure you wish your meeting to follow.

- Whenever possible, make an appointment beforehand rather than turning up unannounced. Cold calling is inefficient, as frequently the person you need to see will be out, in a meeting or otherwise unavailable. In addition, many people are hostile to 'salespeople' who turn up uninvited, and you will have to overcome this initial hostility before you can even think about making a sale.

- If – as recommended – you have an appointment, make every effort to arrive on time. If you are going to be late, phone ahead to warn whomever you are seeing. Even if you are late, don't run upstairs or along corridors. This will make you untidy and out-of-breath, and create an unfavourable first impression.

- On meeting the potential customer, introduce yourself and offer to shake hands. Use the person's name ('Good morning, Mrs Grosvenor'). You will, of course, have confirmed this beforehand, preferably while making the appointment.

- Encourage the customer to talk about his or her needs, as this will allow you to respond in the most appropriate way. Show the customer the benefits your service or product offers, as it is these that the customer buys. For example: 'Using my services will free you to spend more time concentrating on what you do best' or 'Your customers will want to order more of these because they're such good value for money.'

- If your service or product can meet the customer's needs, explain how it will achieve this. On the other hand, if you cannot meet his needs, then say so now. Your credibility will be enhanced, and the customer will be more likely to get in touch with you when he does need what you have to offer.

- If the customer raises objections, listen carefully, making notes if appropriate. Then go through the objections one at a time, showing how you will overcome them. Try to anticipate all the possible objections beforehand and have replies prepared for them. Obviously, your ability to do this will improve with experience.

- When you sense that the moment is right, close (i.e. complete) the sale. Don't risk irritating your customer by carrying on listing benefits once he has definitely decided to buy. Get him to sign an order form if appropriate, and leave a copy, which should include the agreed price.

- Aim to end the meeting on a positive, friendly note. Reassure the customer that he has made a wise choice in deciding to purchase from you. Even if he has not made a purchase on this occasion, you should aim to leave him with the impression of a warm, trustworthy person with whom he would like to do business in the future.

*Telephone selling*

The telephone can be an invaluable tool for selling. It can be used in a variety of ways. In some circumstances you may be able to close a sale directly over the phone, thus saving the cost and time of going to see the customer in person. This is especially the case when selling to former or current customers. More often, however, the telephone will be used in the first stage of the selling process. By phoning a potential customer, you aim to find out: (a) whether the business uses (or might use) the service or product you are selling; and (b) the name of the person who would make the decision on purchasing.

You can then ask to speak to this person and attempt to make an appointment to see him, or alternatively you could write a sales letter addressed to him personally. After a few days, you could then phone to check that he received your letter, and try to make an appointment to see him in person. Using the telephone as part of your sales strategy has the great advantage that it allows you to contact a large number of potential customers, and narrow these down to the most promising 'prospects' on whom to concentrate your personal selling efforts.

Here are a few tips on using the telephone for selling:

(1) Prepare in advance what you are going to say. Write it down and have it in front of you when you pick up the phone to call a potential customer. Practise with a friend or your partner/spouse, or in front of the bathroom mirror. Your aim should be to sound relaxed and natural, not as though you are reading from a script.

(2) Choose the right time to call. With business customers, towards the end of the day when they are winding down may be the best time. If you are calling private individuals, it is preferable to avoid ringing them at work, as they may feel awkward or embarrassed at discussing their personal affairs in front of colleagues. It is best to ring such people at home in the early to middle part of the evening.

(3) When making your call, relax and try to use a normal, conversational tone. Don't worry if you have a local or regional accent – people at the other end often react positively towards this, feeling that the person calling them is more natural and 'real'.

(4) Keep a smile on your face while you are speaking. This will help you relax, and the good humour in your voice will communicate itself to the other person.

(5) Set yourself targets for numbers of calls to make. If you are 'cold calling', there is a good chance that many of the people you phone will be uninterested in what you have to offer. However, if only one in ten wants to know more, this still means that by making 100 calls you should be able to fix up ten appointments.

(6) If the person on the other end is rude or abusive, avoid the temptation to be rude back. Just put the phone down and call the next name on your list. Professional telephone salespeople are trained to welcome every rejection they receive as one step nearer to the next acceptance. It will help greatly if you can adopt a similar attitude yourself.

## After-Sales Service

Making sales is essential to the survival of every business, but the marketing process does not – or should not – end there. Your aim should not merely be to make a single sale, but to create a satisfied customer who will come back to you – perhaps many times – and recommend your business to his friends and relatives.

Your marketing strategy should therefore include some means of ensuring that your customer is satisfied with the service or product he has received, and reassuring him that you will be there to help if any problems arise later. If problems do subsequently occur and you are able to resolve them, this is a powerful means of generating customer loyalty and ensuring your business gains a good reputation.

The kind of after-sales service that is appropriate will obviously differ from business to business, but one measure worth pursuing in many businesses is keeping in regular touch with former customers, even if they haven't bought from you for a while. You might, for instance, write to let them know of any new services you are offering. You could even send out a regular newsletter, or a copy of your latest brochure or catalogue. Another idea which works well in some types of business is to follow up a sale with a reminder of when the procedure concerned is due to be repeated. For example, a mobile mechanic might write to a customer to remind him when his car's next service is due.

Finally, when complaints arise, investigate them thoroughly and accept responsibility if the fault has been yours. If such is the case, offer a refund, replacement or whatever is most appropriate. A customer with a complaint who feels that he has been treated fairly and sympathetically is very likely to become one of your most loyal customers in future. A generous policy here frequently pays huge dividends in long-term customer goodwill and support.

All of these strategies will help improve your business's reputation and build confidence in your product or service. No businessman who hopes to succeed over a period of years can afford to neglect the importance of after-sales service.

## Marketing Awareness

As a small business owner it is important always to be thinking about ways in which your service or product could be marketed better. One method is to observe what others, especially your nearest competitors, are doing, and be prepared to adapt or 'borrow' their best ideas. Listen also to your customers, especially when they ask for a service or product you do not currently provide, and consider whether it would be feasible to offer this. Even if you do not have time for any other market research, by these simple techniques you will stay aware of your market and be able to develop and expand your business.

# chapter 18

## How to get 'free' publicity

As well as paid-for advertising, you may be able to obtain a certain amount of free publicity for your business if you understand and apply the principles of PR (public relations). Although professional PR practitioners will argue that their jobs concern much more than just getting free publicity, for the small home-based business this is by far the most important aspect of PR.

Media coverage obtained through PR is normally free, though it can be time-consuming to arrange. The aim of this approach is to get information about your business into magazines or newspapers in the form of articles or news stories. This can be a very effective way of publicising your business, as people are often more inclined to believe what they read in a news item than in a paid-for advert.

The main way to achieve news coverage is by sending out a press release. This is a short news story that you hope will be published by the paper, or prompt one of their reporters to write an article based on it. Press releases must contain something newsworthy, as newspapers will not simply print a piece saying how wonderful your business is. Nevertheless, local papers in particular are often under-staffed and welcome good stories they can use, even if the news they contain is not particularly earth-shattering. A few events that might justify a press release include:

- the opening of your business
- winning a big order
- winning a prize or award
- celebrating an anniversary
- offering a new service
- developing a new product
- sponsoring a local sports team
- assisting a charity or charitable appeal
- special offers, events, and so on

A press release should NOT be written in the same way as an advert. The idea is to achieve coverage in the news pages, so you should try to imitate the concise, factual style used by newspaper reporters. Your aim should be to produce a story or article that could be used by the editor without requiring any changes. If your press release is published more or less as you wrote it, you can congratulate yourself on a job well done! The main principles of press release writing are summarised below.

(1) On the top of your headed notepaper write the date and the heading PRESS RELEASE in block capitals.

(2) Below this, write a heading for the release. This should explain in a nutshell what the release is about – for example, LITTLETON TOY-

MAKER GETS CONTRACT WITH HAMLEYS! or LOCAL PHOTOGRAPHER WINS NATIONAL AWARD.

(3) Below this, write the text of your press release. As mentioned, this should be in article rather than advertisement style. Aim to answer as concisely as possible the five Ws – WHO, WHAT, WHEN, WHERE and WHY (that is, WHO you are, WHAT you have done, WHEN you did it, WHERE you did it, and WHY you did it). Try to cover all the main points in the first paragraph or two, as the lower half of the release may be cut if the editor is short of space.

(4) If possible, include a quote from yourself or someone else in your business. This can lighten the tone of the release and make it look more like a 'proper' news story (which nearly always include quotes). It will also help greatly if you can include a photograph to accompany the release (or let the editor know that photographs are available on request).

(5) At the end of the release, include a phone number where a reporter can contact you to get more information.

You can send your press release to the editor, or to the reporter who covers small business matters for the paper. Don't expect to succeed every time - your release may be competing with hundreds of others – but when you do manage to get coverage the amount of interest it generates can more than justify the effort you put in. Below is an example of a press release so that you can see what they look like.

PRESS RELEASE

July 3 2008
For Immediate Release

LOCAL PHOTOGRAPHER WINS NATIONAL AWARD

Local photographer Jenny Richardson is celebrating after achieving first place in the Kodak National Photographic Awards, 2007/08. As well as £1,000 worth of photographic equipment, her prize includes an all-expenses-paid trip to South Africa to take pictures of wild animals on safari.

This theme of this year's Kodak competition was 'Plants and Animals', and Jenny's prize-winning photos included a number of her cat, Sylvester, playing in her garden. She will soon be taking pictures of much bigger cats in the famous Kruger National Park.

Jenny's more usual subjects include children and wedding parties. She says, 'Winning this award was a wonderful surprise for me, but I don't intend to become a full-time wildlife photographer. I enjoy working with couples and families in Littleton too much to give that up.'

Would-be clients wanting to book Jenny for a forthcoming wedding or other event can contact her on 0700 344566. Jenny says she will give a 10 percent discount to anyone mentioning that they heard about her through this article.

Further information: Jenny Richards
                    Tel: 0700 344566 (day/evening)

If you find you enjoy writing press releases and have some success with them, you could try your hand at writing short articles, perhaps for trade or technical magazines. You should not necessarily expect to be paid for such articles, but will benefit from the publicity they generate.

## Sales Promotions

Sales promotions are closely related to PR. They are designed to generate extra interest in your product or service, but rather than working via the media they aim to appeal to potential customers directly. A few examples of sales promotions are as follows:

- giving free samples
- discounts for some types of buyer (e.g. students, unemployed)
- free gifts with purchases
- giving talks or demonstrations about your product or service
- special opening offers
- fashion shows
- competitions
- vouchers giving money off the next purchase
- mobile demonstrations
- exhibitions

Sales promotions aim to attract new customers and retain old ones. As you will note from the list above, they allow you to give your creativity free rein. Promotions are often combined with advertising (e.g. you could mention in your adverts a two-for-the-price-of-one offer) and with public relations (e.g. in the sample press release, the sales promotion of a 10 percent discount for every customer mentioning the article was used).

Sales promotions are increasingly popular among businesses, with some finding them more effective for generating sales than traditional advertising. You do, however, need to be careful that you are not giving away money needlessly. The aim of sales promotions should be to attract new customers who then become regular clients. Promotions are therefore best used occasionally rather than continuously, and their effectiveness should be carefully monitored.

# chapter 19

## Book-keeping and accounts

Before you begin trading, it is essential to have a suitable system in place for keeping financial records. Such records are vital, both for the information they can give you about the success (or otherwise) of your business, and when the time comes to prepare your end-of-year accounts.

## The Need for Financial Records

There are many good reasons why businesses need to keep accurate financial records. For one thing, as mentioned above, at the appropriate time you will have to use them to prepare accounts for the tax authorities, so that they (and you) know how much tax you will have to pay. If your accounts do not show clearly what you have earned the tax inspector will make his own estimate, and you may find yourself paying more tax than you should.

Keeping good records is to your own benefit as well. For one thing, they will show you how well or badly you are doing at any given time, so that you will not suddenly find yourself having to sell your business, or even your home, to pay off your debts. Before you spend money, you will want to be sure that you can afford to spend it. If you know about money problems as soon as they arise, you have a much better chance of putting them right before they become too serious.

If you want people to lend money to you, they will certainly expect to see your accounts. For example, a bank will want to ensure that the business is likely to do well enough to pay back any loan, together with interest, within the time specified. Finally, if at some stage you decide to sell your business, any potential purchaser will wish to see the books and accounts.

However small your business, therefore, you must keep accurate financial records. The smaller your business, the simpler these can be, but they must still be accurate, detailed and up-to-date. All bills sent out and received must be carefully filed, and you must be organised and methodical in all your record-keeping.

## Book-keeping Systems

Particularly if you are operating as a sole trader or a partnership, you have considerable freedom of choice in deciding what books to keep. In making your decision, there are a number of factors to keep in mind.

### (1) Simplicity

There is no point in having a system more complex than you require. Especially if you have little knowledge or experience of book-keeping, a simple system such as an analysed cashbook – to be discussed shortly – may be perfectly adequate. In any case, your book-keeping system should be simple enough that you understand it and can easily explain it to someone else if you are away for any reason.

If your books are unnecessarily complex, the danger is that you will spend excessive amounts of time in maintaining them, time you could more profitably use in running your business; or else your books may not be completed fully or correctly, and the information in them will be worthless.

*(2) Legal Requirements*

While simplicity is important, your books and accounts must meet the requirements of business law. In particular, if you have chosen to trade as a limited company, there are quite strict conditions on what records you must keep and when and how you submit your accounts. Your professional advisers (accountant and solicitor) should be able to advise you on these points. If your business is a particularly complex one, or you know that working with figures is not your strong point, it may be advisable to engage a freelance book-keeper to take on this area of responsibility.

*(3) Usefulness*

As already mentioned, one of the most important reasons for keeping financial records is to obtain useful information on which to base decisions. A system that is too complex and difficult to understand may not produce information quickly enough to identify problems or exploit profitable opportunities.

*(4) Professional Advice*

Before making any decision on what book-keeping methods and systems to use, it is highly advisable to consult an accountant. Your accountant will be one of your most important professional advisers, as it is he who will have to translate the information in your books into accounts for the tax authorities. If you consult him at an early stage you can ensure that your systems are set up in the way in which he prefers, and so cut down the time he has to spend preparing your accounts (and hence the amount you have to pay for his services).

## A Simple Book-keeping System – The Analysed Cashbook

This is a simple system that will nevertheless meet the needs of many home-based businesses (during their early years at least). To operate it you will require an analysis book, available from all office stationery suppliers (the system can also be easily adapted for use on a computer with a spreadsheet program – see below). Analysis books are large, hard-backed books, pre-ruled with narrow horizontal lines and up to thirty (or more) vertical columns. You can use one book for income and another for expenditure; or, to economise even further, use the front of your book for expenditure and the rear for income.

The use of the system is best explained using an example. The one used here concerns an individual working as a freelance proofreader and editor; but it would work just as well with the great majority of home-based businesses. The example page below shows how income is recorded. As you will see, the first column is used for the date of each item, and the second for a brief description of the item itself. The next column is then used to record the amount of the item, while the columns to the right of this are used for income in particular categories. The choice of categories is entirely up to you. In the example the three categories chosen are proofreading, editing and sundry income (money from any other source).

| Date | Item | Total | Proofrdg | Editing | Sundry |
|------|------|-------|----------|---------|--------|
| 1/3 | Hodson's | 350 | 350 | | |
| 4/3 | HPI Ltd | 560 | | 560 | |
| 18/3 | Hodson's | 350 | 350 | | |
| 24/3 | XYZ | 50 | | | 50 |
| 27/3 | HPI Ltd | 100 | | 100 | |
| 30/3 | Farmer's | 250 | 250 | | |
| | **TOTAL** | **1660** | **950** | **660** | **50** |

*Record of Income*

As you will notice, each item is entered twice (though this is not the same as double-entry book-keeping!). By totalling up all the columns at the end of each month, you will be able to see the total you have earned that month, and the amount contributed towards that by the different types of income. If you keep a running total from one month to the next, you will be able to keep track of your progress throughout the year, and will have the figures all ready for your end-of-year accounts.

Your record of expenditure would look similar. Again, a simple example is shown below.

| Date | Item | Total | Stationery | Postage | Phone |
|------|------|-------|-----------|---------|-------|
| 3/3 | Stamps | 10.00 | | 10.00 | |
| 7/3 | Phone | 60.00 | | | 60.00 |
| 16/3 | Envelope | 0.45 | 0.45 | | |
| 24/3 | Stamps | 5.00 | | 5.00 | |
| 24/3 | Folders | 8.25 | 8.25 | | |
| 30/3 | Stamps | 20.00 | | 20.00 | |
| 31/3 | Labels | 5.95 | 5.95 | | |
| | **TOTAL** | **109.65** | **14.65** | **35.00** | **60.00** |

*Record of Expenditure*

This method of record-keeping helps you keep track of what you are spending in different categories. For example, in the record above, you can see at a glance that you have spent a total of £35 on postage during March. For practical purposes, there would probably need to be a few more categories of expenditure other than those shown above, including perhaps training, travel, insurance, professional fees and subscriptions, bank charges, and – not least – money you have withdrawn for your own use (usually known as drawings).

To claim an item of expenditure against tax, you should if at all possible get a receipt for it. It would therefore be a good idea to have an extra column on the left-hand-side of the page for receipt numbers. You can number receipts consecutively, starting again from 001 each year. Mark the reference numbers on the receipts as well, so that you have an easy way of identifying which item of expenditure each receipt refers to.

A further refinement is that, instead of the single column for 'Total', you might instead have two columns: one for items paid for out of your business account (by cheque, standing order, etc.), and the other for items paid for in cash. This will make life easier when checking your financial records against your bank statements. And when/if the day arrives when you have to register for VAT (see Chapter 15, *Tax, National Insurance and VAT*) you could simply add further columns to record VAT paid to suppliers and VAT charged to customers.

Although this is a very simple system, it contains all the information that would be required to draw up a set of accounts. This system has been used satisfactorily by the present author for nearly twenty years.

## Using a Computer

If you have a computer with a spreadsheet program, it is easy to adapt the system described above to it. Keeping your books on computer has one great advantage: the computer can do all the calculations for you (e.g. adding up columns and calculating running totals). This can lead to considerable savings in time and effort. Most spreadsheet programs will also allow you to display financial information in the form of graphs and tables, which can be helpful in seeing long-term trends.

The analysed cashbook system can be used with any spreadsheet program, e.g. Microsoft Excel. You can also, however, buy dedicated programs (again based on spreadsheets) on which to keep your financial records. By far the most popular of these in the UK is Microsoft Money. This program includes the facility to download information from your bank account via the Internet (assuming, of course, that you have online banking set up). This can save you time in entering data, and will provide you with a mass of tools for displaying and manipulating financial information. You will still, however, need to do some work to customise the program to your own individual circumstances.

## Submitting Your Accounts

It is, of course, quite possible to prepare and submit your annual accounts to HMRC without involving an accountant. If your annual turnover is below a certain figure (currently £15,000), you do not have to submit detailed information, just figures for your total business turnover and allowable expenses. If you are running your business as a part-time sideline, you may prefer to do this rather than paying an accountant to produce a full set of accounts that are unlikely to be required. Even so, if you do this you should still keep detailed and accurate financial records, both for your own benefit and for calculating the figures for your tax return. Remember, also, that HMRC may decide to investigate your return in more detail (a certain number of taxpayers are randomly chosen for this ordeal each year). In this case you are likely to be required to produce the records from which your income and expenditure figures were compiled.

If you are running a full-time profitable business, you are still of course at liberty to produce your own accounts. However, most self-employed people in this category prefer to pay an accountant a few hundred pounds to handle this task for them. There are many advantages to this, including the following:

- Paying an accountant to do this leaves you more time to concentrate on running your business.
- The accountant will have much more experience of dealing with the tax authorities than you do, and is far less likely to make mistakes.
- If the tax inspector has any queries, the accountant should be able to answer them.
- The accountant may be able to suggest (legal) ways you can reduce the amount of tax you have to pay.
- He or she may also be able to suggest additional benefits and allowances you could be claiming.
- And finally, the tax authorities may be less inclined to query a tax return if they can see that it has been completed by a qualified accountant.

Overall, for most small business owners, trying to do your own end-of-year accounts is likely to prove a false economy. Certainly the great majority, unless they have an accounting or book-keeping background, use a professional accountant to prepare their accounts and handle any negotiations with HMRC. Most accountants, incidentally, will also complete and submit your annual self-assessment tax return as part of their service.

# chapter 20

## Invoicing and credit control

In some businesses (e.g. window cleaning) customers expect to pay you there and then, but in others you will be required to present an invoice. This applies particularly where your customers are other businesses rather than private individuals (e.g. desktop publishing, indexing). Businesses generally require some sort of invoice for tax purposes, and in any event they are often not in a position to hand over money or write out a cheque to you there and then.

An invoice is basically just a request for payment within a specified period (typically 30 days). Newcomers to business are often concerned about this, but there is no need to be. An invoice can be quickly and simply produced on your own letterhead or, at a pinch, a sheet of plain paper. In any event it should include the following items:

- your business name and address
- your phone number (in case there are any queries)
- a reference number (chosen by you)
- the name and address of the organisation being invoiced
- the amount to be paid
- the date

An example invoice is shown below.

---

**JONATHON DOE**
**Website Designer**

101 London Road, Middlewood, Worcs, WR7 9LT.   Tel: 01534 792909

TO: Sunlight Conservatories Limited
Unit 7, Colebrook Industrial Estate
Basingstoke
Hants
RG21 4RY

8 July 2008

**INVOICE NO: P/751**

To design work and consultancy on company website.

20 hours @ £25 per hour

**TOTAL DUE:**
**£500**

Terms : Payment in 30 days
Please make cheque payable to J. Doe

Signed.......................................................

---

*Example Invoice*

The reference you put on the invoice is up to you, but clearly these should follow one another in numerical order. A simple method, as used in the example, is to use a letter (or letters), followed by a number. If you like, the letter could identify the type of job performed – so a mobile mechanic might use an 'S' prefix for invoices referring to servicing, 'R' for repairs, and so on. In any event, it is important to put some sort of reference number, as large organisations in particular often require one for their payment systems. And when in due course you receive payment, frequently the only indication of what it refers to will be the invoice reference number (often written on the back of the cheque or an accompanying 'with compliments' slip).

As soon as you have completed a job you should prepare your invoice and send it by first class post (the sooner your customer receives it, the sooner you can expect to be paid!). Keep a copy of all invoices, and check regularly to ensure they have been paid (see Credit Control, below). If you send out large numbers of invoices to some customers, you may find it desirable to send them a monthly statement listing the dates and amounts of all invoices outstanding. However, for most home-based businesses this is unlikely to be necessary.

If you issue more than a very few invoices, it is best to keep a record in a separate invoice book. This need be no more than a list in numerical order, including the following information:

- invoice reference number
- date issued
- to whom
- amount
- date payment received

You could also include a column in which to record details of reminder letters/phone calls (see below). Checking regularly in your invoice book will help you keep track of accounts that have not yet been paid.

## Credit Control

Most customers will of course pay your invoices within the period specified, but sometimes the required payment fails to arrive. In this case you will need to consider what further action to take.

The best first step, once an invoice is more than a fortnight late, is to phone the debtor up. At this stage you should avoid the least hint of a threat. Your approach should be friendly, your attitude that you are merely 'jogging his [or her] memory' about an overdue payment.

In many cases this will be quite sufficient. There may have been a genuine slip of the memory or, in larger organisations especially, the paperwork may have gone temporarily astray. In such cases, a simple phone call may be all that is needed to jolt someone into action and produce the required payment.

If this still fails to produce a result, your next step may be either a personal visit or a letter. Personal visits can be productive with private individuals in particular, as they may well be embarrassed into paying the bill there and then. However, making a personal visit to a debtor is admittedly not the most appealing of prospects; and if the debtor concerned is on the other side of the country, visiting may not in any event be practicable. In such cases you may decide to write instead. When writing to a company or individual concerning an unpaid debt, follow the guidelines below:

*(i) Be clear and concise*
Many people believe that debt collection letters must be written in legal mumbo-jumbo. That is not the case. State in plain English the amount owed and the goods or services the debt relates to, quoting your original invoice number if relevant.

*(ii) Be firm but polite*
The payment may have been delayed for all sorts of reasons, some perfectly innocent, and you may still want to do business with the debtor again some time in the future.

*(iii) Do not ask why the debt has not been paid*
If you ask this, you are inviting the debtor to come up with an excuse rather than the money he owes.

*(iv) Do not ask for part-payment or payment by instalments*
Doing this immediately puts the idea into the debtor's head. If the debtor subsequently contacts you to suggest such an arrangement, you may have to consider it (even if you reject such an offer, a court is very likely to find it acceptable). However, you should always ask for the whole amount initially.

*(v) Personalise all letters*
Avoid writing to 'The Accounts Department' or 'The Manager'. Try to address all letters to a named individual. Avoid, also, putting 'first reminder' at the top of the letter. This tells the debtor that there are more such letters to come, and he can safely delay payment a bit longer.

*(vii) Write only two letters*
The first of these will set out the debt and request payment, while the second will give warning of legal action if payment does not follow within a specified deadline (say seven days). If the second letter still fails to produce payment, you must then begin legal proceedings (see below).

## Taking a Debtor to Court

If your phone calls, letters and visits still fail to produce a result, you may have to consider legal action. As soon as you start proceedings, however, you will accrue further costs in the form of court fees and (if you engage one) solicitor's bills. Before going any further, therefore, you should check the following points:

(i)   Has the debtor got the money to pay the debt? If not, you are merely throwing good money after bad.

(ii)  Do you have written evidence to support your claim? This will be required by the court, particularly if the debtor disputes the amount outstanding.

(iii) Do you have the full and correct name and address of the debtor? This will be required for the legal forms.

(iv)  Is the debt less than six years old? If it is over that, it cannot generally be recovered.

If you can answer these four questions affirmatively then you can – and should – proceed with legal action. If you back off at this point, the debtor will know that your earlier threats of legal action were empty. Your chances of ever recovering the debt then will be zero.

At this stage you may decide to hand over the case to a debt collector or a solicitor. You should definitely do this if the sum owed is over £100,000 (admittedly this is unlikely for a home-based business), or if there is some dispute over the nature or amount of the debt. In England and Wales you can get a free half-hour consultation with a participating local solicitor under the 'Lawyers For Your Business' scheme. You can get more information about this by phoning 020 7405 9075, or e-mailing lfyb@lawsociety.org.uk.

There is, however, one straightforward method by which a small business owner, even with no previous experience, can pursue a legal case for an unpaid debt. That is by seeking a judgment against the debtor in the county court.

## Making a Claim in the County Court

Claims for debts of under £100,000 are normally dealt with via the county court system in England and Wales (in Scotland and Northern Ireland there are similar procedures going under the name of 'arbitration'). This procedure is designed to be simple enough to be used by people without the aid of solicitors (though solicitors can and do use this method as well).

To begin a case, you will need to attend at your local county court and collect three copies of a form known as a 'default summons'. You should also be given a set of explanatory leaflets explaining what you have to do next. Essentially, you are required to fill in the forms including details of the amount you are claiming and why you believe you are owed this money. You pay a court fee (which is added to the total outstanding) and the summons is then issued. The debtor has a set period (16 days for a limited company, 21 for an individual) either to pay the debt or explain why he disputes it. In the latter case, a date for a hearing is then set at which both sides can present their case in front of a judge, whose decision is legally binding.

Another option for accessing the county court system that has become available recently is to use the HM Court Service Money Claim Online website at https://www.moneyclaim.gov.uk/csmco/index.jsp. This service is available to anyone pursuing a debt of up to £100,000, so long as (a) they have an address in England or Wales where legal documents can be served, and (b) the defendants (the people you are suing) also have an address in England or Wales. Court fees are slightly lower when using the website, and you do not have the hassle of going to court to collect the necessary forms. Obviously, though, you will need a computer with Internet access to use this method.

If the defendant does not dispute the debt, you will almost certainly get a judgment in your favour. If payment is not made within one month, the debt will then be published on the Register of County Court Judgments against the name of the individual or company concerned, and will make it difficult for them to obtain credit in future. Hopefully they will now pay the debt via the court, and in due course you should receive the full amount owed, including any court fees you have had to pay.

If they still don't pay, you will need to think about enforcing the judgment. A full discussion of this is outside the scope of this guide – you really need the help of a solicitor here – but the options will include sending in bailiffs, or even applying to freeze the defendant's bank account. All of these options will involve you in further expense, however – so you will need to weigh up carefully whether you may simply be throwing good money after bad. If a debtor is determined to use any method possible to escape paying, and doesn't care about the damage to his reputation caused by a CCJ, it can be almost impossible to squeeze the money out of him by legal means.

One final point on credit control is that you should keep a close eye on the overall average time taken for your invoices to be paid. If this starts to creep up, it can have a damaging effect on your cashflow, and may ultimately cause your business to fail if for this reason you are unable to meet the demands of your creditors. If certain clients seem to be taking longer and longer to pay, it may be worth making some discreet enquiries to ascertain whether they are experiencing financial difficulties. In any event, you should continue to send them reminders as soon as an invoice becomes overdue. Ultimately, you may need to consider whether you can afford to go on offering credit terms to very slow payers.

# chapter 21

## Insurance

Even if you are running a single-person business from home, you are likely to require additional business-related insurance. At the very least, you should check whether you need to amend your home contents and buildings insurance.

At one time home insurance companies often refused to cover items such as personal computers if they were used for work purposes. Some insurers still take this attitude, but a growing number are more enlightened. In fact, there seems little reason why insurance companies should discriminate against home-workers, as the fact that they are around during the day should actually reduce the likelihood of burglaries and other disasters.

It is particularly important to notify your home insurance company if your business uses expensive equipment or supplies, or if valuable stock will be kept in your home. If you fail to notify your insurers, they may refuse to pay out if these items are damaged or stolen. Upgrading from am ordinary home contents policy to a business policy is not expensive, and in most cases should cost only a few extra pounds a month.

Apart from home insurance, other types of business-related insurance you may require according to your particular circumstances include the following:

*Public liability* – This provides you with protection if a member of the public suffers injury, loss or damage caused by defects in your products, services or premises, or by the negligence of you or your employees. Any business dealing with the public should have public liability insurance, though it is not legally compulsory.

*Employer's liability* – This is similar to public liability insurance, but covers you for claims from your employees. In Britain public liability insurance is generally compulsory if you employ staff or you are a director of a limited company (in which case you are considered an employee of the company). It is not legally essential for sole traders and partnerships with no employees. Nevertheless, it may still be prudent to take out an employer's liability policy, in case an accident occurs when a friend or relative is helping you. You should also bear in mind that a self-employed sub-contractor working on your behalf may be considered as your employee for insurance purposes.

*Business interruption* – This provides cover if for some reason you are unable for a period to go on running your business. The circumstances causing this might include a break-in, computer failure, ill health, call for jury service, or sudden family crisis. Business interruption cover compensates you for the loss of income during this period and the possible loss of clients and contracts.

*Personal accident/disability insurance* – This will ensure your future financial security in the event of you suffering a disabling illness or accident. This is particularly important for sole traders and those with family responsibilities who have no other source of income should they become unable to work.

*Motor vehicle insurance* – If you intend to use your private car or van for business purposes, you may well find that an ordinary domestic insurance policy will not cover it. If your business will involve transporting other people's goods, you are likely to need an additional 'goods in transit' policy to cover the goods while they are in your possession.

*Credit insurance* – Insuring against bad debts can be expensive, but is worth considering if most of your business will be done with just a few large companies. What would happen to your business if one of these customers suddenly went into liquidation owing you large amounts of money?

A broker will be able to advise you on your insurance requirements; plenty are listed in Yellow Pages. The services of such individuals are usually free, but most are paid by commission on the policies they sell, so it is in their interests to persuade you to buy as much cover as possible. You will therefore need to weigh up their advice carefully and buy only as much insurance as you need and can sensibly afford. This is obviously something of a balancing act, and it is desirable to review the position every year as your business develops and changes.

Finally, a quick word should be said about The Lark Group, an independent UK broker specialising in insurance for home-based businesses. The Lark Group offers a range of home insurance policies which also incorporate the additional cover many home-based businesses require. Their Homeworkers Policy, for example, includes along with the usual buildings and contents insurance, public liability, employer's liability, business money and contents, personal accident, and business interruption cover. Further information is available from The Lark Group on 020 8557 2424, or their website at www.larkinsurance.co.uk.

# chapter 22

## Where to get more help

As the preceding sections have indicated, running your own business demands a range of knowledge and skills quite apart from those required to make your product or deliver your service. As a business owner you inevitably have to be something of a 'Jack of all Trades'. This means not only exercising a broad range of skills, but also recognising situations where it is necessary to seek advice and assistance from outside advisers. This section will highlight a number of advisers whose help you are most likely to find useful.

## Accountant

A good accountant can be invaluable in setting up and running a successful business. Among the wide range of services available from accountants are the following:

(1) advice on the most appropriate legal and financial structure for the type of business you are starting
(2) advice on possible sources of additional funds
(3) advice on what books to keep and (if required) doing the book-keeping
(4) preparing financial accounts and tax returns
(5) liaising and negotiating with the tax authorities
(6) advice on future financial planning to minimise your tax liability
(7) advice and assistance with controlling creditors and debtors (credit control)
(8) general financial advice, for example with regard to loans and subsidies, grants, pension planning, and so on

In addition, for small limited companies, an accountant will undertake work concerning the formation of the company, the issue and transfer of shares, annual returns, auditing the company accounts, arranging Annual General Meetings, and general company secretarial work (often in conjunction with a solicitor). Many small companies also use their accountant's address as their registered office.

Finally, a good experienced professional accountant may be an invaluable source of general management advice, particularly for sole traders who may otherwise feel rather isolated when making decisions on the running of their business.

Of course, it is not essential to engage an accountant when first starting out, particularly if you have a knowledge of book-keeping and accounts yourself. On the other hand, you will almost certainly need help from an accountant at some stage, especially regarding such matters as VAT registration and dealing with the taxman. For some of the (many) other reasons why you should consider engaging an accountant sooner rather than later, see Chapter 19, *Book-Keeping and Accounts*.

*Choosing your accountant*

The first step in choosing an accountant is deciding what you want from him (or her). Not every accountant will offer every sort of service. For example, large city firms are unlikely to offer a weekly book-keeping service, while a sole practitioner may not have the expertise to help with raising capital or setting up a limited company.

Large accountancy firms serve mainly medium to large-sized businesses, and their fees are often high. For an individual starting a home-based business and wanting someone to prepare their accounts and provide general financial advice, a partnership or sole practitioner will often be the best choice. There is a good argument for choosing a partnership rather than a sole practitioner, as there is always a chance that the person concerned will fall sick, move away or even die, leaving you without anyone to handle your accounts. With a partnership, at least if one partner moves on there will be someone else in the business to take over.

Before choosing an accountant, ask around for recommendations, e.g. from other people you know who run their own businesses. Contact a number of accountants, whether or not they have been recommended to you, and ask about their terms. Ask for details of existing customers who would be willing to provide references, and get in touch with these people. Finally, bear in mind that anyone can call himself an accountant, so check that the person you wish to appoint has the appropriate professional qualifications.

*Cost*

How much an accountant will cost depends on the type and amount of work involved, and this can be difficult to predict in advance. Nevertheless, most accountants will give you an estimate. For a straightforward service involving preparation of accounts and occasional financial advice, most will charge you a single annual fee. For a small home-based business, you should expect to pay somewhere in the region of £300 to £600.

Many accountants spend much time and effort just sorting out their clients' financial records, and the cost of this inevitably has to be passed on. It therefore pays to set up a book-keeping system your accountant is happy with, and keep it neatly and accurately. An hour of the accountant's time spent discussing what books you are going to keep now may save him having to spend many hours later sorting through your records.

## Solicitor

Whilst most businesses require the services of an accountant on a fairly regular basis, assistance from a solicitor will generally be needed only when a specific problem or query arises. Situations in which you might need the advice and help of a solicitor include:

(1) deciding the most appropriate structure for your business
(2) drawing up a partnership agreement
(3) buying a business
(4) evaluating and purchasing a franchise
(5) forming a limited company
(6) legal aspects of employing staff
(7) health and safety requirements
(8) collecting unpaid debts
(9) selling your business

In addition, a solicitor is likely to be needed when a trading agreement has to be drawn up (e.g. an import/export deal or joint trading arrangement with another company). For the benefit of all parties involved, such agreements are usually formalised in legal contracts. Your solicitor will help to draft such contracts, ensuring that they are acceptable to everyone concerned and comply with all the legal requirements.

Finally, businesses may use the services of solicitors when a dispute arises. If one business decides to sue another in court (e.g. for unpaid debts or infringement of a patent), a solicitor will usually be engaged to handle this.

*Choosing your solicitor*

Similar principles apply when choosing a solicitor as with an accountant. Solicitors specialise in different aspects of the law, and you need to choose one with expertise in industrial and commercial matters rather than a specialist in, say, criminal or family law. Most solicitors operate in partnerships, and often there is one partner who specialises in business matters. You should aim to meet this person and satisfy yourself that he has the experience and knowledge you require. As when choosing an accountant, it is wise to take up references

*Cost*

Whereas your accountant may charge you an annual fee, a solicitor is likely to charge you for each job you want doing. Before engaging a solicitor, you should ask him for an estimate of costs. If the solicitor says that this is not possible because he does not know how long the job will take, ask him for his daily rate. Many solicitors will quote a package price for certain jobs such as forming a limited company.

To keep costs under control, it is important to give your solicitor clear instructions, and ask him to keep you informed of the costs incurred in any ongoing action. In disputes between businesses, in particular, legal costs can quickly mount up.

## Other Sources of Help

In addition to the advisers described above, there is a range of others you may be able to call upon as circumstances dictate. The main ones likely to be relevant to home-based businesses are listed below.

*(1) Bank manager or bank business adviser*

You might not immediately think of your bank manager or bank business adviser as one of your professional advisers. That is because, unlike most other advisers, you do not pay directly for their services (you pay indirectly, of course, in the form of bank charges). Nevertheless, such individuals can be a source of advice on a wide range of business matters.

As someone with a close knowledge of what other local businesses are doing, the manager or business adviser will be well placed to comment on your plans and make suggestions on how they could be improved. Like an accountant, he should be able to advise you on many of the financial and managerial aspects of your business. Many banks also offer advice on matters such as insurance, investments, pension planning, and so on.

A bank manager or business adviser is not a substitute for an accountant, however. For one thing, while your accountant will give you objective, impartial advice, the bank manager's advice is bound to be influenced to some extent by the fact that he sees you as a (potential) client and source of revenue for his bank. In addition, you may not always wish to discuss business problems with someone from your bank, in case (for example) this influences their decision on whether to give you a loan.

Finally, it is worth noting that while some banks still offer business advice at branch level, in other banks services to businesses have been centralised in large call centres. If your account is held with such a bank, you will lose the advantage of local knowledge that a manager or business adviser in branch can provide. Before choosing a business banking provider, therefore, this is certainly something you should consider.

## (2) Insurance broker

As explained in the previous chapter, every business needs insurance. Its basic purpose is to reduce the risk of calamitous loss in some unforeseen misfortune befalls you or your business. Some insurance is essential and legally compulsory, while other types are desirable so long as you can sensibly afford them.

An insurance broker will advise you on the most appropriate insurance for you and your business. He will negotiate on your behalf with insurance companies to arrange the best deal for you. Insurance is a highly specialised area, and a professional insurance broker can be of great assistance in cutting through the jargon and choosing among the many types of policy and cover on offer.

Insurance brokers do not normally work for any particular insurance company and so, in theory, will give you independent advice. However, they are usually paid by commission, so it is in their interests to sell you as much insurance as possible. When dealing with insurance brokers, therefore, it is important to weigh up the advice you are given against how much you can sensibly afford to spend.

## (3) Advertising agent

The job of an advertising agent is to help businesses advertise their products or services. An agent will first advise you on your advertising policy in general. He will design and write your advertisements – in consultation with yourself – and book space for them in appropriate publications. Agents will also produce and book advertisements for other media such as radio when required.

Advertising agents receive commission from the publications in which they place advertisements, so their charges for this type of work are generally quite reasonable. Most agents will also assist with other types of publicity such as press releases and publicity brochures. Higher fees may be payable for this type of work, as the agent does not recoup any of his costs in the form of commission.

For small local businesses whose advertising amounts to no more than the occasional classified ad in their local paper, an advertising agent is unlikely to be required. If you plan to advertise more widely, however, using the services of an advertising agent is highly recommended. A number will be listed in your local Yellow Pages. Call a few and explain the type of business you are in and the level of advertising support you require. The agency will tell you soon enough whether they are able to assist you; if so, you will be invited in to discuss your requirements in detail with one of their executives.

*(4) Designer/graphic artist*

If your business will involve producing or selling a product or products, you might wish to hire a designer to advise you on matters such as colour, shape, features and so on. A graphic designer, otherwise known as a commercial artist, can help with tasks such as designing your logo and letterhead, creating an 'image' for your business, preparing attractive packaging material, and so on. Graphic artists and designers normally charge an hourly fee.

*(5) Website designer*

As mentioned in Chapter 14, *Computers and the Internet*, a growing number of small businesses are creating websites as a means of advertising themselves and communicating with their customers. It is actually not difficult to produce a basic website yourself if you have some degree of computer knowledge, but for anything more ambitious (and especially if you hope to sell directly from your site) it is wise to engage a professional website designer. Such individuals advertise in local papers and Yellow Pages (look under Internet Services). They will normally quote you a set fee (starting at around £200) for designing your website and installing it on the web. You will have to pay a further sum to have your site regularly updated.

*(6) Business consultants and advisers*

There is a huge range of specialists who will offer advice on various aspects of your business. Probably the most relevant to the new small business are the advisory services set up and operated by government agencies in the hope of encouraging new business development and creating employment and wealth. One such, mentioned earlier in this book, is the Business Links network. Business Link is a government-funded service designed to promote enterprise in England. Local Business Link organisations provide support, advice, services and information to anyone planning to set up a business in their area. To be connected to your nearest Business Link centre, phone 0845 600 9 006, or see www.businesslink.gov.uk. If you live in Scotland, Wales or Northern Ireland, the following national organisations should be able to help:

Scotland: Business Gateway – 0845 609 6611 – www.bgateway.com
Wales: Business Eye – 08457 96 97 98 – www.businesseye.org.uk
Northern Ireland: Invest NI – 028 9023 9090 – www.investni.com

## Using Your Advisers

To make the best use of your professional advisers, bear in mind the following points:

(1) In the end it is still you who will have to make the actual decisions. For example, you must decide whether to sue a particular debtor – your solicitor can advise you on the procedures.

(2) Most professional advisers charge according to the amount of time they spend working for you. To make the most economic use of their services, therefore, you should do as much preparatory work as possible. With your accountant, for example, you should ensure that your books are properly completed and balanced before passing them over to him to produce your final accounts.

(3) Your professional advisers are also in business to make money. In choosing your advisers you should therefore apply the same care and judgment as when you are buying any other product or service. This includes getting estimates of fees and 'shopping around' before committing yourself.

With any adviser it is best to keep the relationship on a friendly but professional level, with each party having respect for the other's position. If you do not feel comfortable with an adviser, or do not feel you are getting the service you expected, then make arrangements to change to someone else.

Good advice is, however, well worth paying for, and often results in savings or extra income worth many times the fees charged. Advisers' fees, incurred for advice solely in connection with the business, are of course allowable as a tax-deductible item of overhead expense.

# chapter 23

## Expanding your home-based business

Follow the advice in this book and, with just a little luck as well, your home-based business should soon be thriving. Initially you may not have enough work to keep you occupied the whole time, but within a few years – perhaps sooner – you may find yourself with more orders than you can fulfil (at least, to the standard you would wish). At this point you will face a tricky decision.

A.  Start turning down offers of work, and risk causing resentment and losing money, or

B.  Take on someone to assist you, either an employee or one of the other options discussed later.

Deciding whether to expand your business can be tricky, and often the choice boils down to why you decided to become self-employed in the first place. If your main motive was to make money, the argument for expansion may be hard to resist. On the other hand, if you started your business primarily to fit in with your domestic circumstances or as an enjoyable sideline, you may prefer to continue as you are and forgo the financial benefits of expansion. In any event, it is important to be aware of the pros and cons.

## The Advantages of Expanding Your Business

As a one-person business, your income potential is automatically limited by the number of hours you as an individual have available. Even if you decide to work 90 hours a week, every week (not recommended, for the sake of your health!), in the end this is all the time you have available. If there is more work than you can cope with in this time, the only way you will be able to complete it is if you have one or more people to help you. So long as the amount you earn from their efforts is more than the amount they cost, their contribution will add to your business profits. This may be best illustrated by an example.

## EXAMPLE

Marco is a self-employed builder. In his first year he does a total of 1,470 hours of chargeable work at £15 an hour. This means that his gross income is 1,470 x 15 = £22,050. From this he has to deduct fixed costs of £5,000 (all his variable costs such as materials he charges to customers). This gives him a net profit before tax of £17,050.

As he has plenty of work in hand, at the start of his second year Marco takes on an assistant, Carol. He pays her £6 an hour, and charges customers for her work at £11 an hour. In his second year Marco's income from his own chargeable work to customers is again £22,050, but in addition he is able to charge customers for 1,600 hours of Carol's time at

£11 an hour. This brings in another £17,600, giving him a total gross annual income of £39,650. Of course, Marco has to pay Carol a wage, which, as she works 35 hours a week with paid holidays, comes to 52 weeks x 35 hours x £6 = £10,920 a year.

Marco's fixed costs increase to £7,000 due to the additional expenses such as employer's national insurance he incurs by taking Carol on. Nevertheless, at the end of the year his net annual profit before tax is £39,650 (gross income) – £10,920 (Carol's wages) – £7,000 (overheads) = £21,730. In other words, employing Carol increases Marco's annual net profit by nearly £4,700.

---

The above example illustrates the principle that employing people can make you money. There are, however, two important riders. One is that you must have sufficient work to occupy both yourself and your employees, or you risk paying them but not earning anything from them. And secondly, the amount you charge customers for your employees' time must more than cover the cost of their wages and any additional costs that employing them entails. The difference between what your employees cost you and what you can charge for their time is the contribution that employing staff makes towards paying for your overheads and ultimately adding to your profits.

One other point is that, although making more money is usually the main incentive for expansion, another may be to avoid disappointing customers and potential customers. As your business becomes established, your existing customers, seeing that you are a reliable supplier, may begin to place larger orders. Meanwhile, new customers will keep coming to you from different sources, including word-of-mouth recommendation. To cope with all this extra demand and avoid turning potential customers away (people whose custom you might welcome in a few months' time if business takes a downturn), you may well have to give serious consideration to expansion.

## Drawbacks of Expansion

Expanding your business has many attractions, especially in financial terms. However, it does have one or two possible drawbacks, and it is important to take these into account when deciding how to proceed. The main drawbacks of expansion are loss of control, greater administrative demands and higher risk.

*(1) Loss of control*

Expanding your business is likely to involve taking on staff or partners, and you will inevitably have to delegate some of your responsibilities to them. Some of the time it may be these people who are dealing with customers rather than yourself, and they may not always give as good a quality of service as you would like. As the business grows, there will be more people involved in it, and even if they are paid employees rather than equal partners, you will still need to pay some attention to their views. You will not have the same freedom of action that you may have had as a one-person business.

*(2) Greater administrative demands*

As the business grows the administrative demands inevitably increase. If you take on employees, for instance, dealing with their tax and national insurance contributions (as well as your own) will inevitably take up a proportion of your time. It may be possible to delegate some of these responsibilities to other staff or professional advisers, but you are still likely to find yourself spending more and more time doing this type of work. Of course, if you enjoy administration and management, this may not be a problem.

*(3) Greater risk*

As the business expands the sums of money involved will become larger, and, so inevitably, will the risks. If you take on staff, you will need to ensure that there are sufficient orders to keep them all in work; if there are not, you will have to face the unpleasant prospect of laying them off.

It is quite likely that you will have to borrow money to finance your expansion. If the business subsequently fails, the debts you owe to banks, suppliers, staff and so on will be that much larger. Keeping such risks under control involves careful financial planning, and monitoring your business's actual performance against predictions. It may also involve changing to a different form of business organisation, such as a limited company.

### Alternatives to Employing Staff

If you don't want to take on an employee, there are various other options you could consider, at least in the short term.

*1. Involve your partner*

The obvious person to turn to for help initially is your partner or spouse. Even if they do not have your specific work-related skills, they may be able to assist with the administration, thus freeing you to spend more time on paid work for customers.

Paying your husband or wife a fee for their assistance can also have tax advantages, particularly if they do not have any other source of income. The reason for this is that the money you pay them can be set against their annual tax-free personal allowance. If you do this, however, the Inland Revenue may want to see proof that they do actually provide services to the business.

*2. Involve other members of your family*

It may also be possible to involve other close family members, e.g. your parents or teenage children. Care may be needed here, however. Teenage children, especially if they are unemployed, may resent being pushed into a career they have no interest in. And parents may find it difficult to accept the role reversal which being your 'employee' entails. If, however, you have a good relationship with the relatives concerned and they seem genuinely eager to play a part, involving other members of the family in your business can offer many potential advantages.

*3. Use an employment agency*

Particularly if you need help for short spells only, using a 'temp' from an agency can be an attractive option. The agency will take care of all the administration for you and simply invoice you for the temp's time. Of course, you will also have to pay the agency a fee for their service, and this can be quite substantial. Agencies can provide temporary staff in most office-related fields, e.g. clerical, word processing, book-keeping and so on. Some agencies can also supply labourers, drivers, assembly workers and other manual staff.

*4. Use an office services bureau*

Office services bureaux provide a wide range of office-related services for small businesses, including book-keeping, accounts, telephone answering, word processing, handling post, and so on. They can also perform tasks such as maintaining databases, producing address labels and filling envelopes for mailshots. You can call by in the morning with the day's assignments, and again in the evening to collect the finished work and any messages that have arrived for you. Offices services bureaux are listed in Yellow Pages under the headings Secretarial Services, Telephone Answering, and so on.

*5. Sub-contract some of your work*

Sub-contracting is common in certain trades and professions. Basically it involves passing over some aspects of a job to someone with similar (or complementary) skills. A builder, for example, may sub-contract some types of work (e.g. plastering or bricklaying) to other self-employed people who can do the job faster and/or better than he can, so that his own time can be used more efficiently on other matters. In this situation the builder would typically invoice the customer for the whole cost of the project, and pay the sub-contractor out of this.

Sub-contracting can be used in a wide range of spheres, including some with which it is not traditionally associated. The present author, for example, has successfully sub-contracted some parts of guidebooks he was commissioned to write to people living in the countries concerned who had better first-hand knowledge of these places than he did.

*6. Take on a partner*

Finally, you could take on someone else as a partner in your business. This can work very well if your partner has similar but complementary skills. For example, a 'stills' photographer might form a partnership with someone else who specialises in videography, so that between them they can offer a full range of photographic services. Note that your partner need not work from the same premises as you. Each could continue to work from his/her own home, but using a common business name and administrative facilities. If you decide to go into partnership with someone, it is strongly advisable to have a formal partnership agreement drawn up by a solicitor. You should also speak to your accountant concerning the book-keeping and tax implications.

## Final Thoughts

As your home-based business takes off, you are likely to find yourself needing good administrative and organisational skills, as well as the skills required actually to provide your product or service. This applies especially if you decide to expand by taking on staff and/or a partner. This will inevitably involve you in a greater degree of administration and management, and a greater burden of responsibility (see below). You will need to plan ahead, both on a long-term and short-term basis, to ensure that you use your working time and resources as efficiently as possible. You will also need to monitor your business's performance carefully to ensure that you are not in danger of over-reaching yourself.

Expanding your business can boost your income to far higher levels than you could ever achieve as a one-person operator, but it also imposes a greater burden of responsibility – not only on yourself, but on your family and any employees or partners. If you prefer to keep your home-based business small, therefore, you should not feel that this is an admission of failure. As stated earlier, the decision on whether or not to expand is a highly personal one, very much dependent on your own aims and ambitions in running a home-based business. If you are happy as a 'one-(wo)man-band' and willing to forgo the potentially much higher earnings you might achieve in an expanded business, then continuing as you are may well be the right decision for you.

Good luck, and enjoy running your home-based business!

# chapter 24

## Home-based business profiles

In this 'bonus' chapter I've set out details of over fifty home-based business opportunities. Some of these are jobs you can do at home, while in others you will be working on clients' premises and simply using your home as a base. But all of these businesses can be started and run from home – none needs separate premises (at least, until the time comes when you want to expand).

It's worth noting that some of these jobs are likely to require specialist training (unless you already work in the field in question). Others, though, are open to anyone to start almost immediately. Where training is likely to be necessary, I have included information on training providers and/or organisations who should be able to assist you.

The profiles are arranged in alphabetical order. For each one the nature of the work is described in brief, together with resources for finding out more. The opportunities listed are by no means the only ones open to home-based workers, but they cover a broad range. If you are still struggling to come up with a suitable idea for your business, I hope they may inspire you and open your eyes to a few possibilities you might not otherwise have thought of.

## 1. Alternative/Complementary Therapies

Alternative therapies (also known as complementary therapies or medicines) have grown in popularity in recent years. The term covers a wide range of approaches, but one thing they all have in common is an emphasis on treating the whole person. Most practitioners place as much importance on mental and spiritual well-being as they do on physical illness. Just a few of the better-known alternative therapies include acupuncture, reflexology, aromatherapy, homeopathy and phytotherapy (medical herbalism).

Courses in alternative therapies can be taken by almost anyone. Unlike conventional medicine, where qualification requires five years or more, many fields of alternative medicine do not require lengthy training. There are some exceptions to this, however. For example, to achieve a recognised qualification in homeopathy, students have to complete a rigorous training course of three or more years' duration.

At present most alternative therapies are not subject to official regulation; for example, anyone can set up in business as an aromatherapist or reflexologist without necessarily possessing any relevant skills or qualifications. In future, however, many of these specialisms are likely to become subject to legal regulation; and it is in any event important from both a personal and a business point of view not to skimp on the required training.

*Further Information:* A good place to start is The Institute for Complementary and Natural Medicine (ICNM). This was formed in 1982 to provide the public with information on complementary medicine. The ICNM also administers the British Register of Complementary Practitioners. You can obtain information from them on approved training courses in many forms of complementary medicine.

The Institute for Complementary and Natural Medicine
Can-Mezzanine
32-36 Loman Street
London
SE1 0EH
Tel: 020 7922 7980
Web: www.i-c-m.org.uk

## 2. Babysitting

You won't get rich as a babysitter, but it can be a relatively easy way of earning a part-time income. To babysit very young children, you will need some relevant experience; and many of the agencies which supply babysitters insist on their sitters having some form of childcare qualification. There is no minimum legal age at which you may babysit, but most agencies require you to be over 18.

*Further Information:* There are no legal regulations for babysitting as there are for childminding, and no central body for either babysitters themselves or babysitting agencies. However, many local education authorities run courses for teenage babysitters, and the Royal Society for the Prevention of Accidents (RoSPA) puts out some useful leaflets.

Royal Society for the Prevention of Accidents
Edgbaston Park
353 Bristol Road
Edgbaston
Birmingham
B5 7ST
Tel: 0121 248 2000
Web: www.rospa.com

## 3. Beautician/Beauty Therapy

If you enjoy looking good and helping others do the same, this could be the ideal opportunity for you. You can work from your own home, in clients' homes, or (one or two days a week perhaps) in an upstairs room at a local hairdressing or beauty salon. If you decide to work from a room in your own home you are likely to need planning permission. Some authorities may also require you to register with them, depending on the range of services you intend to offer.

Beauticians offer a variety of beauty treatments, including depilatory waxing, eyebrow shaping, eyelash and eyebrow tinting, facials, manicures, pedicures, nail extensions, and so on. Beauty therapists traditionally offer a wider range of treatments, including some which are primarily concerned with promoting health and fitness rather than beauty as such. In recent years the distinction between beauticians and beauty therapists has become increasingly blurred, and nowadays the term beauty therapist is increasingly applied to anyone working in this field.

In theory, men can be beauty therapists as well as women, but in practice (for obvious reasons) the great majority are female. With modern men becoming increasingly concerned about good grooming and health, however, opportunities for men in this field look set to increase.

*Further Information:* The main organisation serving and representing beauty therapists in the UK is the Guild of Professional Beauty Therapists. They provide a range of services for their members, including professional indemnity insurance (essential in this occupation), legal and business advice, and the bi-monthly journal Guild Gazette. The Guild can also provide details of organisations offering training in beauty therapy across the UK.

The Guild of Professional Beauty Therapists
320 Burton Road
Derby
DE23 6AF
Tel: 0845 21 77 383
Web: www.beautyguild.com

## 4. Book-Keeping

With more and more people setting up their own businesses, the demand for freelance book-keepers has never been greater. Keeping the books is one of those tasks many businessmen and women hate – yet it is essential to keep financial records, both for the taxman and to see how well the business is doing. Many business people are therefore more than happy to pay a freelance book-keeper to take care of this task for them, while they concentrate on doing what they do best.

Freelance book-keepers work mainly for self-employed individuals and small businesses. They ensure that all receipts and outgoings are correctly entered in the business's books (though most businesses today use computers rather than the traditional books or ledgers). They may also compile monthly management accounts, and handle matters such as VAT, wages, bank reconciliations (checking bank statements against the information in the business's books), and so on.

They may also be engaged on a short-term basis by larger firms, who may need assistance in preparing a report for HMRC or some other agency. Book-keepers do not, however, normally prepare a business's final (end-of-year) accounts, as this is the province of an accountant.

*Further Information:* The main professional body in this field is the International Association of Book-keepers (IAB). Becoming an IAB member entitles you to a range of benefits, including a bi-monthly magazine, subsidised courses and seminars, professional indemnity insurance schemes, and so on. IAB Members who have completed the Association's qualifying examinations and have at least two years' practical experience are entitled to use the letters MIAB (Member of the International Association of Book-keepers) or FIAB (Fellow) after their name.

Most colleges run book-keeping and accounting courses, many of which can be taken as short courses or evening classes. A range of correspondence courses is also offered by the National Extension College (NEC).

The International Association of Book-keepers (IAB)
Burford House
44 London Road
Sevenoaks
Kent TN13 1AS
Tel: 01732 458080
Web: www.iab.org.uk

The National Extension College
Michael Young Centre
Purbeck Road
Cambridge
CB2 8HN
Tel: 01223 400 200
Web: www.nec.ac.uk

## 5. Car Cleaning and Valeting

In recent years car cleaning and valeting has been something of a growth area. Many people want to keep their cars in 'showroom condition', but lack the time, the inclination and (probably) the skills to do it themselves. They are therefore happy to pay a professional car valeter to do the job for them. If you want a healthy outdoor occupation and enjoy working with cars, this could therefore be a good opportunity for you.

At the most basic, you could offer a straightforward cleaning service. Armed with no more than a bucket, a sponge and a chammy leather, plus a bottle of wash-and-wax, you may be able to find a steady trade among householders willing to pay a few pounds for the convenience of having their car washed for them. On the other hand, most areas nowadays have an automatic car wash nearby – and you may also face accusations that you are stealing business from the local scouts! If you want a full-time business rather than merely a sideline, offering a full car valeting service is likely to be a better bet.

Car valeting involves doing much more than a simple wash. A full valet might include all the following treatments: shampoo the vehicle; clean the wheels; wash the bodywork and wheel arches; de-grease and polish the door hinges; remove any stains and deposits; polish with long-lasting wax; shampoo the seats, carpets, mats and boot; clean and condition plastics, bumpers and dashboard; clean the windows inside and out; condition leather; clean the engine bay and spare wheel compartment; repair minor scratches; and deodorise the vehicle. A full valet is a painstaking process likely to take at least an hour-and-a-half, perhaps longer if the vehicle is in a very dirty condition.

If your house has a suitable front or back yard, you could operate from here. This is, however, the type of business your neighbours could well take exception to, and planning permission could be an issue. A better option might be to operate a mobile valeting service.

*Further Information:* Training courses in car valeting are offered at many local colleges. They tend to be aimed mainly at people employed by garages and valeting companies, but there is no reason why a self-employed person could not enrol on them. Courses typically run one day a week, and lead to qualifications such as an NVQ or SVQ in vehicle valeting.

## 6. Carpet and Upholstery Cleaning

This business deals with the types of cleaning which are not generally covered by the ordinary domestic/office cleaner – items which need cleaning only at fairly long intervals. If you choose to stick to the domestic market you will have to seek new customers constantly, as you are unlikely to visit each home more than once a year. Adding 'disaster restoration' (cleaning up after fire or flood) to your repertoire will enable you to get work from insurance companies.

This is a business that requires a fair amount of know-how to understand how best to tackle any given type of fabric and stain, and the right equipment and chemicals. You will also need a suitable vehicle to transport these materials, which will not easily fit into the average car. If you do not choose to invest in the necessary machinery immediately, most of it is available from hire shops, but the cost of hiring will obviously make a large dent in your takings. If buying, expect to pay around £600 for a basic cleaning machine.

There are numerous franchised operations such as Servicemaster and Safeclean, which offer a full business package, including all the necessary equipment and supplies of chemicals, plus full training and marketing support. These typically require an initial investment of over £10,000.

*Further Information:* The British Institute of Cleaning Science offers training and advice on the latest developments in cleaning chemicals and their use.

British Institute of Cleaning Science
9 Premier Court
Boarden Close
Moulton Park
Northampton
NN3 6LF
Tel: 01604 678710
Web: www.bics.org.uk

For more information about franchising as a route into running a home-based business, see Profile 20.

## 7. Children's Entertainment

If you enjoy being with children and have the skills and personality to keep them amused for an hour or two, being a children's entertainer could be both fun and profitable for you. The main demand is for people who can provide entertainment at birthday parties for children typically between the ages of four and ten.

Most children's entertainers have a range of skills. They organise their 'shows' in a series of varied sessions to cope with young children's notoriously short attention spans. These might include joke-telling, magic, Punch & Judy, face painting, balloon modelling, juggling, stilt walking, children's discos, sing-songs, party games, competitions, and so on. Another popular activity at parties held in the summer is an inflatable such as a 'bouncy castle'. Some entertainers specialise in one particular field, most commonly magic (conjuring).

*Further Information:* There is no shortage of books available to help you learn basic children's entertainment skills. Some adult education centres offer courses in circus skills (juggling, stilt-walking, unicycle riding, etc.). A number of companies sell conjuring books and equipment by mail order or via the Internet. One such is The Magic Company, which sells a wide range of tricks and accessories via its website at www.themagiccompany.co.uk.

## 8. Childminding

Childminders look after other people's children in their own home. With an ever-increasing number of women wanting or needing to go out to work, the service is in considerable demand. Childminding is by no means an easy option, but if you enjoy the company of children and are healthy, energetic, adaptable and not too houseproud, you may find this an enjoyable and fulfilling way of making a living.

Childminders do far more than simply watch over their charges. They provide a safe but stimulating environment, with plenty of opportunities for the children to learn through play. They also take them out from time to time, e.g. to a local park or playgroup. They provide meals as required, and supervise games and activities. Childminders must be registered with the local authority, and are subject to an annual inspection.

*Further Information:* Your local Children's Information Service (CIS) can provide potential childminders with information and support about becoming registered, and many also run training or taster courses in childcare. Contact ChildcareLink on 0800 2 346 346 or www.childcarelink.gov.uk to get contact details for all local CIS's.

The National Childminding Association (NCMA) is a membership organisation for childminders and others involved in providing daycare for young children. They offer an advice and information service, and have a network of local groups.

The National Childminding Association
Royal Court
81 Tweedy Road
Bromley
Kent
BR1 1TG
Tel. 0800 169 4486

## 9. Home/Office Cleaning

Cleaning other people's homes, or offices and shops, is one of the easier businesses to get into. There has always been, and will always be, a big demand for people to do this work. The work is not highly paid, but if you go on to establish a cleaning business, with your employees doing the actual cleaning, your earnings can be much higher.

As well as regular cleaning, you could also offer a spring-cleaning or 'just moved into a new home' service. These tasks can be combined with furniture, carpet and curtain cleaning services, which you can either do yourself (hiring the equipment as and when you need it) or by working with specialist cleaners who provide these services but do not do 'ordinary' cleaning.

*Further Information:* The British Institute of Cleaning Science offers training and advice on the latest developments in cleaning chemicals and their use.

British Institute of Cleaning Science
9 Premier Court
Boarden Close
Moulton Park
Northampton
NN3 6LF
Tel: 01604 678710
Web: www.bics.org.uk

There are many franchise opportunities available in the home/office cleaning field. For more information about franchising as a route into running your own business, see Profile 20.

## 10. Computer Installation and Maintenance

Over five million computers are sold every year in the UK, many of them to people who have little or no prior knowledge of computing. An opportunity has therefore opened up for people with a good practical knowledge of computers to offer an installation and maintenance service. There is in fact a wide range of related services you could offer, including installation, repairs and problem-solving, upgrades (e.g. adding more memory or setting up a wireless network), and even computer cleaning.

*Further Information:* There is no shortage of books covering the skills required in this occupation. A number of computer-related distance-learning courses are offered by International Correspondence Schools (ICS). Their range includes a computer repair and upgrading course. You can contact them by phone on 0800 056 3983 or via their website at www.icslearn.co.uk.

## 11. Computer Programming

Computer programmers make their living writing the step-by-step instructions computers use to perform their tasks. Relatively few freelances write machine code (the deepest level of instructions used by computers for their internal operations). Most home-based freelances are applications programmers. They help their clients customise standard 'off-the-shelf' programs so that they meet the specific needs of the business concerned. Most freelances have a particular area in which they specialise, e.g. accounts packages or databases. Some freelances possess specialist knowledge of one or more computer languages, e.g. C++ or Visual Basic.

*Further Information:* One well-established provider of distance learning courses in programming and related skills is Computeach International. They offer a wide range of courses, including programming, systems analysis, networking, database management, and so on.

Computeach International
University House
Jews Lane
Dudley
West Midlands
DY3 2AH
Tel: 0800 083 0261
Web: www.computeach.co.uk

The leading organisation for people working in the computer industry in the UK is the British Computer Society. Membership is available at various levels based on experience and successfully completing the Society's examinations. Members receive benefits including discounts on books and computers, meetings and special events, a bi-monthly newsletter, and so on.

The British Computer Society
First Floor, Block D
North Star House
North Star Avenue
Swindon
SN2 1FA
Tel: 01793 417417
Web: www.bcs.org.uk

## 12. Computer Training

In recent years computers have been appearing everywhere: in homes, in schools, in business and in government. The pace of change has been so fast that many people have found they need help getting up to speed with the new technology. An opportunity has therefore opened up for freelance computer trainers who can run courses and provide instruction on a range of subjects, including word processing, desktop publishing, the Internet, accounts packages, databases and presentation software.

Freelance trainers provide instruction for both small groups and individuals. They design and run training sessions and courses, typically of one to three days' duration. Courses may be provided to introduce people to computers and specific computer applications, or to improve their existing skills. Trainers prepare a training plan, create handouts and other course materials, and deliver the actual training.

Training sessions for individuals are generally delivered at the student's home, probably using his or her own computer. Another approach is to book a suitably equipped room in a school, college or adult education centre, and advertise courses direct to the public. You may also be able to obtain work from companies and other large organisations, in which case the client will normally arrange the training room and facilities.

*Further Information:* The Institute of IT Training is the UK's leading organisation serving and representing computer trainers. Members receive a range of benefits, including professional recognition, a library and resource centre, a free subscription to the Institute's magazine IT Training, and networking opportunities through local and regional groups.

The Institute of IT Training
Westwood House
Westwood Business Park
Coventry
CV4 8HS
Tel: 0845 0068858
Web: www.iitt.org.uk

## 13. Craft Work

At a time when most high street shops stock only cheap, mass-produced items, many of which are imported from the Far East, genuine hand-made products are becoming more and more popular and are fetching a premium price. To find out exactly what items sell best, you need to visit some craft fairs – items on sale will include patchwork quilts, knitted garments, turned wood items, candles, musical instruments, jewellery, decorated eggshells, ceramics, toys, wickerwork, carvings, and many more. Another aspect of craft work is that of restoration, and this can include anything from restoring antique toys and musical instruments to stained-glass windows.

*Further Information:* There are numerous magazines on each type of craft work, and many book publishers who produce books on crafts. One of these is the Guild of Master Craftsmen; they also offer membership and assistance to craft workers. Don't forget, either, your local library, which should have a good selection of craft books, including some which are no longer available through bookshops. The Crafts Council can provide advice and information on setting up a craft business.

The Guild of Master Craftsmen
166 High Street
Lewes
East Sussex
BN7 1XU
Tel: 01273 478449
Web: www.guildmc.com

The Crafts Council
44a Pentonville Road
London
N1 9BY
Tel: 020 7806 2500
Web: www.craftscouncil.org.uk

## 14. Curtains and Loose Covers

Although both curtains and loose covers are widely available in the shops, good quality versions are not so easy to come by. Neither, if you are not that way inclined (and many people are not), is the ability to know what will suit any given home and its occupants, and this is where you can come in. Many people prefer to have their home re-curtained without the hassle of having to measure up themselves or worry about rings or rufflette tape. They also like to have curtains which suit their style of living and personality, and loose covers to match. Customers are prepared to pay a good price for this service, but in return they do demand top-quality workmanship.

*Further Information:* There are many magazines for home-makers and interior designers, and of course there will be books in your local library to help you with the technical aspects. There are also City & Guilds courses available in upholstery and soft furnishings throughout the country. Further advice and information is available from the Association of Master Upholsterers and Soft Furnishers.

Association of Master Upholsterers and Soft Furnishers
Francis Vaughan House
Q1 Capital Point Business Centre
Capital Business Park
Parkway
Cardiff
CF3 2PU.
Tel: 029 2077 8918
Web: www.upholsterers.co.uk

## 15. DIY and Odd-Jobbing

There are many little jobs that need doing around the modern home, from fixing dripping taps to putting up shelves, not to mention the nasty ones like cleaning out drains and gutters. While many people are willing and able to do these jobs for themselves, others (including many older people) are not, and are happy to pay someone else to get them done.

Although this is usually thought of as a man's business, there is no reason why a competent woman should not do it. Many women, especially the elderly, are unsure of inviting men into their homes but would be happy to engage a female DIYer.

*Further Information:* There are numerous books and magazines covering DIY tasks around the home. College and adult education classes are widely available in subjects ranging from bricklaying to electrical wiring, plastering to interior decorating. A number of Internet sites also offer step-by-step advice on a range of DIY tasks (see, for example, www.diyfixit.co.uk).

## 16. Driving Instruction

With over three-quarters of a million people reaching the age of seventeen each year and so becoming eligible to drive, there is never any shortage of work for qualified driving instructors. If you enjoy driving and don't mind sitting in a car for hours on end, becoming an instructor could be a satisfying and rewarding business for you. The work involves bringing students from beginner stage up to a standard where they can pass the national driving test. Some instructors also offer more advanced tuition, e.g. for the Institute of Advanced Motorists' tests.

As a driving instructor, you can either run your own business or work for a school such as BSM which employs self-employed instructors on a franchised basis. In the latter case you will receive marketing and administrative support from the school, and in most cases use of a vehicle, in exchange for a weekly franchise fee. BSM engage both full-time and part-time instructors.

*Further Information:* The Driving Standards Agency has overall responsibility for driving tests and driving instruction in the UK. People wishing to learn more about becoming an approved driving instructor (ADI) are advised to obtain a copy of the ADI Starter Pack, which tells you everything you need to know before starting instructor training. The pack – for which a small fee is payable – includes the necessary documents to apply for registration.

Driving Standards Agency
Berkeley House
Croydon Street
Bristol
BS5 ODA
Tel: 0300 123 9000
Web: www.dsa.gov.uk

The UK's largest driving school, with around 2,000 self-employed driving instructors on its books, is BSM. They also offer training courses for the DSA examinations, and ongoing professional development and support for instructors. More information is available from their website at www.bsm.co.uk, or you can phone them on 08457 276 276.

## 17. Desktop Publishing

Modern technology has made it possible for individuals to design and produce highly professional-looking documents on computer. Desktop publishing, or DTP for short, eliminates many of the stages required in the traditional publishing process. What's more, the advanced software now available means that you no longer require years of training and experience to get presentable results.

There is a huge market for DTP services among businesses and other organisations. The range of documents you may be asked to produce is equally varied, spanning logos and letterheads, business cards, press advertisements, leaflets and brochures, posters, newsletters, reports, price lists, and presentation materials of all kinds. In today's highly competitive marketplace, crudely typed and photocopied documents are no longer acceptable. Printed materials of all kinds are expected to look good and be produced quickly.

With the wide range of work on offer, some desktop publishers choose to specialise in a particular field, e.g. newsletters. Others enjoy working on a variety of different projects. Whichever path you choose, running your own home-based DTP business can be both creative and fulfilling, though sometimes (with tight deadlines the norm) quite highly pressurised.

*Further Information:* If you wish to study for a qualification in this field, enquire at your local college regarding part-time courses. Distance learning courses in desktop publishing and related fields are available from various providers. One is the National Extension College (NEC), which offers courses in desktop publishing, design and editing, as well as a range of home-study courses on computing.

The National Extension College
Michael Young Centre
Purbeck Road
Cambridge
CB2 8HN
Tel: 01223 400 200
Web: www.nec.ac.uk

## 18. Event Planning/Organising

This can cover anything from organising a son or daughter's 18th birthday party up to major corporate hospitality events with several hundred guests. For private customers, the event will usually be associated with a birthday, anniversary, wedding or some other celebration such as passing exams. For corporate customers, the event might also be an anniversary, e.g. of the company's founding. It could equally be a new product launch, a corporate hospitality event, a sales conference, an annual general meeting, an incentive event for successful salespeople, or a prize jaunt for competition winners. Your customers will be people or businesses who have neither the inclination nor the time to do their own organising. For corporate customers, it often costs less to use an event planner than to get their own staff to do the necessary work.

*Further Information:* The company Event Management Training runs training courses in event planning in London, Manchester, Newcastle, Birmingham, Liverpool, Cardiff, Glasgow, and Edinburgh. They also run distance-learning courses.

Event Management Training Ltd
Premier House
77 Oxford Street
London
W1D 2ES
Tel: 020 7659 2060
Web: www.eventtr.co.uk

## 19. Food Preparation and Sale

There are many possibilities in the food and catering business. They include specialising in wedding cakes; cooking for dinner parties, cocktail parties or directors' lunches, either in your own kitchen or your customer's; and selling home-made cakes and preserves on a market stall. In general it is best to concentrate on some sort of speciality such as cordon bleu cookery, canapés or finger food for parties, wedding/birthday cakes, or the new growth areas of vegetarian and organic food.

*Further Information:* Trade magazines such as The Grocer, Caterer & Hotelkeeper and Independent Caterer will give you a good idea of what is happening in the food and catering industry right now. The Food Standards Agency issues several useful booklets, including 'Starting Up: Your first steps to running a catering business' (also available to download from their website).

Food Standards Agency
UK Headquarters
Aviation House
125 Kingsway
London
WC2B 6NH
Tel: 020 7276 8000
Web: www.foodstandards.gov.uk

## 20. Franchising

Franchising isn't a business in itself, but rather a method of 'buying in' to a business brand and format devised by someone else. With a franchise you typically pay the franchisor an up-front fee, and possibly additional fees once you're up and running as well.

Franchising has become a very popular method for getting started in business. It has the great advantage that you aren't starting from scratch. In exchange for your fee, you will normally get a ready-made (and hopefully proven) business format, along with training, materials, assistance with marketing, and access to advice and support any time you need it.

Of course, some franchises are better than others, and it's very important to research any franchise that interests you carefully. Find out as much as you can about it, and in particular try to speak to some existing franchisees to get their impressions. Be wary of franchises based around a current fad which may no longer be marketable in a year or two's time. Look for proven, successful business concepts for which – as far as you can tell – there will always be plenty of demand.

Some franchises are unsuitable for operating from home – those that require retail premises, for example. But that still leaves a good number that can be run in this way, at least initially. Most of the business profiles listed in this chapter – and many others – are available as franchises.

A franchise for a home-based business will typically cost you from £5,000 to £50,000. This is clearly a substantial sum, though finance may be available from the franchisor (or elsewhere). If you like the idea of starting your own business but don't want to do it all yourself, buying into a good franchise has much to recommend it.

*Further Information:* The British Franchise Association is the voluntary self- regulating governing body for franchising in the UK. They arrange one-day introductions to franchising at venues across the UK, where you can meet and talk to franchisors, franchisees, legal professionals, and so on. Information about the current schedule can be found on the BFA website. This also lists all franchisors belonging to the Association, along with links to their websites so that you can find out more about them.

British Franchise Association
A2 Danebrook Court
Oxford Office Village
Langford Lane
Oxford
OX5 1LQ
Tel: 01865 379892
Web: www.thebfa.org

It's also worth looking out for the The Franchise Magazine, a glossy monthly publication sold in shops and available free online. This has articles on all aspects of franchising, and every issue lists hundreds of current franchise opportunities. You can view their website at www.thefranchisemagazine.net.

## 21. Gardening

If your garden grows better than that of any of your neighbours, you might consider using your 'green fingers' as the basis for a profitable business. Chances are that if you're a keen gardener you already have most of the equipment you need, so all you will require is some method for transporting this and you're in business. Another attraction of gardening is that, once you have built up a group of clients, they will want you back at regular intervals to keep everything looking spick and span.

*Further Information:* The professional association for people working in this field is the Institute of Horticulture. The Institute provides a range of services for its members, who include garden designers, landscape contractors, private and local authority gardeners, and so on. Different grades of membership are available depending on experience and qualifications. More information is available on the Institute's website at www.horticulture.org.uk.

## 22. House-Sitting Service

A combination of high boarding costs for pets, rising crime rates, and a general reluctance among householders to leave their homes empty when going away has led to a great demand for house-sitters. These are people who move into a home while the owners are away to look after the place, tend the garden and care for any pets. Sitters don't themselves earn a great deal and many are retired people (though sitters for agencies that specialise in larger or more exotic animals such as horses or farm animals can be as young as 25). If you want to earn a full-time income in this business you will probably need to run an agency providing sitters rather than acting as one yourself.

*Further Information:* The Home Service offers a nationwide house-sitting service; as a means of gaining experience, you may wish to contact them to offer your services.

The Home Service
Unit 4, Potkins Lane
Front Street
Orford
IP12 2SS
Tel: 08451 303100 or 01394 450865
Web: www.housesitters.co.uk

## 23. Indexing

Some indexers work in-house in publishing houses, libraries and other organisations, but the majority are home-based freelances. The work involves preparing indexes not only for books but for magazines and journals (single issues or volumes), audiotapes, films, computer disks and other information sources.

*Further Information:* The main organisation serving and representing indexers in the UK is the Society of Indexers. Members receive the Society's journal The Indexer and its quarterly newsletter Sidelights, and can attend regular meetings, conferences and short courses. The Society runs an open learning course for new indexers, for which members receive a discount.

The Society of Indexers
Woodbourn Business Centre
10 Jessell Street
Sheffield
S9 3HY
Tel: 0114 244 9561
Web: www.indexers.org.uk

## 24. Interior Design

Interior design is one of the growth areas of recent years. With the high cost of buying and selling property, more and more people are deciding to redecorate or re-model their homes instead. Many people decide to tackle the work themselves, but around one in seven gets help from an interior designer. In addition, a growing number of businesses want their premises to be given the 'designer touch'. All this adds up to good news for people with the aptitude and skills to become freelance interior designers.

*Further Information:* The main professional association for people working in this field is the British Interior Design Association (BIDA). The Association provides a range of services for its members. It also offers a free matching service for potential clients looking for a designer in their area. Different grades of membership are available depending on experience and qualifications.

British Interior Design Association
BIDA Ltd
Units 109-111 The Chambers
Chelsea Harbour
London
SW10 0XF
Tel: 020 7349 0800
Web: www.bida.org

## 25. Internet Auction Trader

The Internet has created many opportunities for home-based workers, but one that has become extremely popular is trading on Internet auction sites such as eBay (www.ebay.co.uk). Internet auction traders typically bulk-buy products from wholesalers and sell them individually on the auction sites, hoping to make a good overall profit. They may also seek out 'bargains' on the sites (or elsewhere) which, using their trading experience and expertise, they can then sell on profitably.

Most Internet auction traders specialise in a certain field. This could be almost anything, including fashion, computers, jewellery, antiques and collectables, sporting memorabilia, toys, watches, games, photographic equipment, and so on. There are many advantages to specialising, including learning the true value of products in your niche, finding good sources, discovering what sells and what doesn't, and so on.

One big attraction of becoming a home-based Internet auction trader is that you can easily start part-time and build up to working full time if you wish. Many people start by selling items they already own but no longer require, which does not usually generate any tax liability. This can be a great way of 'learning the ropes' before you launch your Internet auction trading business formally.

*Further Information:* Introductory courses on using Internet auction sites (usually eBay) are available at some local colleges and adult education centres. One useful guide to setting up a UK-based Internet auction trading business is 'Starting a Business on eBay.co.uk for Dummies' by Dan Matthews and Marsha Collier (Wiley). There is also plenty of useful information on the auction sites themselves.

## 26. Introduction Agency

Introduction agencies provide a popular means for unattached people to meet others of like mind. At one time agencies suffered from a certain stigma, but with soaring divorce rates and the increasing isolation of modern life, their role in society has become increasingly accepted. Running an introduction agency today can be a profitable and fulfilling home-based business. Starting from scratch in this field can be difficult, as to arrange suitable matches you will need to build up a good-sized pool of clients quickly. There are various franchises which can make this process easier (though at a price). One example is Top Match, who have a website at www.topmatch-international.com.

*Further Information:* The main organisation representing introduction agencies in the UK is the Association of British Introduction Agencies (ABIA). To join you will have to pay an annual fee and adhere to the Association's code of practice. One benefit of joining ABIA is that your agency will be included on the list sent to people who contact ABIA requesting details of its member agencies. You will also be able to state that your agency is an ABIA member on your publicity materials, thus reassuring potential members that you take seriously your responsibility to provide a good service.

The Association of British Introduction Agencies
Suite 109
315 Chiswick High Rd
Chiswick
London
W4 4HH
Tel: 020 8742 0386
Web: www.abia.org.uk

For more information about franchising as a route into running your own business, see Profile 20.

## 27. Laundry Service

Although many clothes and pieces of domestic linen are supposed to be drip-dry and non-iron, there is nothing as nice as crisply ironed sheets and shirts – as long as you don't have to iron them yourself. So, at least, think many modern householders. Which is why ironing and laundry service businesses are on the increase, and why there is still plenty of room for new ones to start up.

There are three possibilities here. You can either go to your customer's own home and deal with their laundry there, get them to drop it off at your premises and collect it again later, or offer a collection and delivery service as well. You can just do the ironing part, but doing the washing as well does put a stop to arguments about how items have come to be stained.

*Further Information:* The Textile Services Association offers an information service to laundries and other related businesses.

The Textile Services Association
7 Churchill Court
58 Station Road
North Harrow
Middlesex
HA2 7SA
Tel: 020 8863 7755
Web: www.tsa-uk.org

## 28. Leaflet and Newspaper Distribution

If you want a business which provides exercise and fresh air, and are not too concerned about amassing a fortune, leaflet and newspaper distribution could be the opportunity for you.

In recent years there has been a huge growth in the number of items stuffed through letterboxes. Leaflets are particularly popular with local businesses as a means of bringing their products and services to the attention of potential customers. As well as shops and supermarkets, businesses regularly using this method of advertising include estate agents, restaurants, doctors and dentists, travel agents, health clubs, taxi firms, tourist attractions, garden centres and a wide range of other service businesses. Most areas are also served by one or more free newspapers, and someone has to deliver each issue, week in, week out. This can therefore be another regular and reliable source of income.

Although distribution work in itself is not highly paid, if you become a team leader supervising others the rewards are greater. You might also decide to set up your own leaflet distribution agency, employing other people to do the actual letterbox-stuffing, in which case the potential earnings are greater still.

*Further Information:* The best way to learn about this business is to do it, perhaps initially working for a local business or free newspaper. You can check how some established distribution agencies operate by looking at their websites. For example, West London Promotions provide a distribution service for leaflets, circulars and catalogues in the West London area and parts of Surrey and Middlesex. Their website is at www.westlondonpromotions.co.uk.

## 29. Life Coaching

A comparatively new profession which began in the USA, life coaching involves helping people achieve success in their personal and professional lives. This may entail face-to-face meetings, but in many cases is done by regular phone calls. Coaches help people first to understand what they want from life, and then direct and support them as they formulate and follow a plan to achieve their goals.

*Further Information:* Training courses in life coaching and related subjects (e.g. coaching small businesses), including free introductory mini-courses, are run by The Coaching Academy.

The Coaching Academy
39-43 Putney High Street
London
SW15 1SP
Tel: 0208 789 5676
Web: www.the-coaching-academy.com

## 30. Mail Order

Mail order is really a method of trading rather than a business in its own right. A huge range of goods can be sold in this way, from designer tee shirts to garden tools, video games to birthday cakes! Because in this type of business all transactions are done via the post, there are huge savings on premises, staff and so on. Many thousands of mail order businesses are run very successfully by individuals from their own homes. Nowadays they are often based around an 'e-commerce' website, which can be set up quite easily and cheaply. You can then attract customers by promoting your website and/or sending out mailshots to people who may be interested in what you have to offer.

Products most suitable for sale by mail order are those which cannot easily be bought locally (e.g. novelty items, speciality foods, items for collectors and hobbyists, designer fashions, and so on). Some other products also sell well by mail order, e.g. goods for the elderly/infirm, and goods of a personal nature which people may be embarrassed to ask for in a shop. One of the best mail order sellers is information. This can take various forms, including books, magazines, manuals, DVDs, and even correspondence courses. Items which, generally speaking, do not sell well by mail order are heavy, bulky products (too expensive to post), fragile items, awkwardly shaped items, and items which are readily available through shops and other outlets.

*Further Information:* There are various books and distance-learning courses on starting and running a mail-order business. 'Start Your Own Mail Order Business' by Rich Mintner (Entrepreneur Press), while an American title, comes highly recommended. If you plan to base your business around a website, 'Starting and Running an Online Business for Dummies' by Dan Matthews and Greg Holden (Wiley) will provide much of the background information you need. A twelve-part distance-learning course 'Mail Order Business Secrets' is available from Maple Academy (tel. 0800 542 8555 or online at www.mapleacademy.com).

## 31. Modelling

You don't have to be Kate Moss to make money as a model. All types of people are needed, including tall people, short people, fat people, 'ordinary' people, and even ugly people! There are also agencies needing people to model specific parts of their anatomy (mainly the hands and feet). You can earn good money from modelling, even on a part-time basis, and it can also be great fun, giving you the chance to rub shoulders with famous film and TV stars.

A note of caution is in order, however. Some less reputable 'agencies' charge aspiring models large sums of money up front and then fail to make any effort to promote them. Be sure to check out any model agency carefully before parting with any money.

*Further Information:* The Association of Model Agents represents the leading model agencies in the UK. They do not have a website, but if you send them a large, stamped addressed envelope they will send you a list of their member agencies.

The Association of Model Agents
122 Brompton Road
London
SW3 1JD
Tel: 020 7584 6466

## 32. Painting and Decorating

Most people today expect to live in a nicely decorated home. Many are prepared to do their own painting and decorating, but a high proportion are happy to pay someone else to do the work. Even those who are willing to do their own interior decorating will get a professional to repaint the outside of their house, and you may find that much of your work is exteriors. It is, however, not wise to specialise exclusively in exteriors, as this work is very seasonal and dependent on good weather.

*Further Information:* There are City & Guilds courses available in painting and decorating throughout the country. The Painting and Decorating Association offers advice on starting and running a decorating business, and they also negotiate with suppliers to provide discounts for their members. Membership has the added benefit of providing you with the respectability which will reassure potential customers.

Painting and Decorating Association
32 Coton Road
Nuneaton
Warwickshire
CV11 5TW
Tel: 024 7635 3776
Web: www.british-decorators.co.uk

## 33. Party Plan Selling

This is a business where you demonstrate and then sell goods to small groups of people in a private home, taking a commission on every sale. The home-owner is called the hostess (they are almost always female) and the other people are her neighbours and friends. The hostess invites her guests to a 'party' at which she provides tea and coffee (or sometimes wine) and snacks to provide the party atmosphere. In return for hosting the party, the home-owner receives a gift from the parent company. The thinking behind party plan selling is that it allows the guests plenty of time to handle and try the products in a relaxed atmosphere, which they can't always do satisfactorily in a shop.

Probably the best-known example of party plan selling is Tupperware, the kitchen equipment manufacturer, but there are many others, including companies selling books, photograph albums, fashion jewellery and accessories, 'adult' products, diet and health foods, skin care and cosmetics, and even energy products and services (gas and electricity).

*Further Information:* The Direct Selling Association (contact details in Appendix: Useful Organisations) produces a free booklet which lists all its members, with a note of which ones operate using party plan. This will give you a good idea of the range of products sold by this method, as well as providing the necessary contact details. This information is also available via the DSA website at www.dsa.org.uk.

## 34. Personal Fitness Trainer

If you are physically fit yourself and would enjoy helping others achieve a similar condition, this could be the ideal opportunity for you. Personal fitness trainers design workout routines for individuals and small groups. They guide their clients through these routines three or four times a week, either in their own homes or in a gym. As well as exercise plans, trainers also advise and assist clients with other aspects of their lifestyle, most notably their diet. For many clients the main aim is to lose weight, and diet and exercise both play a very important part in this.

*Further Information:* Personal fitness trainers need to have experience in fitness instruction and, in most cases, qualifications. More information can be obtained from the Register of Exercise Professionals (REPs). REPs maintains a register of trained and qualified fitness instructors.

Register of Exercise Professionals
3rd Floor, 8-10 Crown Hill
Croydon
CR0 1RZ
Tel: 020 8686 6464
Web: www.exerciseregister.org

## 35. Pet Boarding

Many people who like animals find themselves looking after their friends' or neighbours' animals at holiday times. It is a small step from here to thinking of turning a favour into a business, but one that should be considered carefully before actually doing it. There are various regulations with which you must comply, including the Pet Boarding Establishments Act, the Diseases of Animals (Approved Disinfectants) Order, various other health and safety requirements from your local council and, of course, planning permission. If you are prepared to negotiate all these hurdles, however, and are willing to invest in the necessary accommodation and supplies for your 'guests', there is considerable satisfaction in pet boarding, and a steady demand for the service from pet owners.

*Further Information:* The Feline Advisory Bureau offers a detailed booklet called 'Starting a Boarding Cattery', and also general assistance. There is no similar organisation for dogs, although the Kennel Club may be able to point you in the right direction. Otherwise, buy some of the many magazines published for pet owners and study the advertisements for animal housing, feed and bedding supplies.

The Feline Advisory Bureau
'Taeselbury'
High Street
Tisbury
Wiltshire
SP3 6LD
Tel: 01747 871872
Web: www.fabcats.org

## 36. Photography

There are two sorts of photography for money. The first is where you are commissioned to produce prints of your work which you sell to the people in the pictures or the owners of the items portrayed. The subjects could be wedding pictures, studio portraits, or even photographs of people's houses, cars or animals. This type of photography is known as social photography.

The other sort of photography is where your work ends up in newspapers, magazines, on the Internet, or perhaps as posters or postcards. What you sell is the right to reproduce the picture, not the ownership of the picture itself, which remains yours. You can sell this right for any given picture many times over.

Whichever type of photography most appeals to you, it is best to have a speciality. This is partly because you will learn what sort of pictures sell best and how to take them, and partly because most people, whether private individuals or professional editors, prefer to use a specialist photographer.

*Further Information:* The Bureau of Freelance Photographers offers various services to its members, including a monthly newsletter which includes market information, an advisory service, and special offers of equipment at discount prices. It also publishes the annual 'Freelance Photographers Handbook', which is available in bookshops to non-members. The Handbook gives details of many magazines and newspapers which use freelance photographers' work, and also lists a range of photographic suppliers and services.

The Bureau of Freelance Photographers
Focus House
497 Green Lanes
London
N13 4BP
Tel: 020 8882 3315
Web: www.thebfp.com

## 37. Picture Framing

Picture framers enhance paintings, drawings, photographs and similar items by mounting them in an attractive, well-made frame. Picture framing is a craft-based service for which there is a steady demand. If you enjoy – and have an aptitude for – woodwork and art, this could be the perfect home-based business for you.

*Further Information:* Part-time courses in picture framing are run at many local colleges and adult education centres. One institution that regularly offers short courses is Barton Peverill College in Hampshire.

Barton Peverill College
Chestnut Avenue
Eastleigh
SO50 5ZA
Tel. 023 8036 7200
Web: www.barton-peveril.ac.uk

## 38. Private Investigation

If you're looking for a slightly offbeat opportunity which nevertheless offers good profit potential, private investigation might be just the business for you. The range of assignments taken on by private investigators is surprisingly wide. Just some of the tasks they perform include tracing missing persons, surveillance, debt collecting and repossession, insurance investigations, 'vetting' employees and potential employees, personal protection (bodyguard) work, process serving (delivering legal documents), statement taking and reporting, and store detective work.

Of course, not all investigators perform all these tasks, and (especially if you live in a well-populated urban area) it is quite possible to specialise in one or more fields which interest you the most.

*Further Information:* The two leading UK organisations for private investigators are the Institute of Professional Investigators (IPI) and the Association of British Investigators (ABI). The IPI offers Membership and Fellowship status for applicants with appropriate qualifications and experience. They also run vocational training courses. The ABI offers a range of useful publications, including 'An Introduction to Private Investigation', 'The Process Servers' Guide', and 'Advanced Surveillance'. They also publish a quarterly journal called Investigate.

The Institute of Professional Investigators
Runnymede Malthouse
off Hummer Road
Egham
Surrey
TW20 9BD
Tel: 0870 330 8622
Web: www.ipi.org.uk

The Association of British Investigators
295/297 Church Street
Blackpool
Lancashire
FY1 3PJ
Tel: 0871 474 0006
Web: www.theabi.org.uk

## 39. Proofreading and Copy Editing

If you frequently find yourself noticing grammatical mistakes in books, magazines and newspapers, proofreading and/or copy editing could be a suitable home-based business for you.

Proofreaders perform a final check on the text of books and other written documents before they are sent to be printed. They mark up any errors they find using a standard set of proofreading marks. These corrections are then incorporated by the typesetter before the book goes to print.

Copy editors are involved at an earlier stage of the publishing process. They work with the author's original typescript. As well as correcting spelling and punctuation mistakes, their task also includes correcting grammatical errors, eliminating bias or possible libel, and generally polishing the text so that it reads well and conforms to the publisher's house style. Copy editing is a more creative task than proofreading, and also more demanding. Many home-based freelances start off as proofreaders and perhaps graduate to copy editing later.

*Further Information:* The professional organisation for proofreaders and copy editors is the Society for Editors and Proofreaders (SfEP). Members receive a monthly newsletter called Editing Matters, and discounts on training courses and publications.

Society for Editors and Proofreaders
Erico House
93-99 Upper Richmond Road
Putney
London SW15 2TG
Tel: 020 8785 5617
Web: www.sfep.org.uk

## 40. Renting Rooms or Property

If you have a spare room in your house, you can turn it into a money-spinning business by renting it out to a lodger. The good news is that the government lets you earn up to £4,250 a year (about £82 a week) in rental income free of all tax under the 'Rent a Room' scheme. If your rental income exceeds this figure, you can opt to pay tax on the balance over £4,250 or pay tax on your net profits after all expenses are deducted. You can choose which of these two options to take every year, depending which is the more financially advantageous for you.

A more lucrative alternative to renting a room is offering bed-and-breakfast. This obviously has most potential in seaside and other tourist areas, though there is also likely to be some demand near major exhibition and conference facilities. If your home is large enough you could even consider turning it into a guest house or hotel, offering evening meals and other facilities such as a bar and games room. This is likely to involve making structural alterations to your property, however, and the legal requirements are more stringent, requiring the assistance of a solicitor.

*Further Information:* Information on the Rent a Room scheme is available from any HMRC tax or enquiry office. Details can also be viewed on the HMRC website at www.hmrc.gov.uk.

## 41. Teaching English as a Foreign Language (TEFL)

With factors such as the opening up of eastern Europe and the growing pre-eminence of English as the world-wide language of commerce, the demand for qualified teachers of English as a foreign language has never been greater.

You can teach English on a one-to-one basis in your home (perhaps combining this with renting a room) or in one of the many specialist language schools in and around London and the regions. This is an ideal-part time occupation which can easily be fitted in with other (e.g. family) responsibilities. It also opens up the possibility of travelling to other countries across the world, where trained and experienced English language teachers are in high demand.

*Further Information:* One institution offering courses in teaching English as a foreign language is ITC. Their intensive weekend courses are designed to provide the basic skills needed to teach conversational English anywhere in the world. This can be followed up with an optional distance-learning course, which leads to the award of an officially accredited TEFL certificate.

ITC
26 Cockerton Green
Darlington
Co. Durham
DL3 9EU
Tel: 08456 445464
Web: www.tefl.co.uk

## 42. Teleworking

Teleworking (or telecommuting as it is sometimes called) involves working remotely from an employer using the phone and new technology (including the internet). There are an estimated 250,000 teleworkers in the UK today, most of whom work from home. Some are self-employed, while others are employees whose employers have made special arrangements to allow them to work in this way.

Teleworkers include a wide range of occupations. Among the most common are software developers, data inputters, website designers, researchers, consultants, writers, charity workers, salespeople, accountants and solicitors. Many large employers now allow some of their staff to work from home; the Automobile Association, Lloyds TSB and British Telecom are three organisations employing significant numbers of home-based teleworkers. A particular growth area at present is 'virtual call centres'. This involves people working from home answering telephone calls to company helplines, support desks, sales enquiry numbers, and so on.

*Further Information:* The Telework Association is a national organisation for teleworkers. Members receive a weekly email bulletin and a bi-monthly electronic magazine called Teleworker. The Association also publishes 'The Telework Handbook', which covers such areas as company schemes, union agreements, business ideas, marketing, insurance, health and safety, equipment, training, and so on. Members receive the book free, or it can be ordered separately from the Association. You can contact the Telework Association by phone on 0800 616008, or via their website at www.telework.org.uk.

## 43. Tourist Guide

As a tourist guide, you will spend your time conducting groups of tourists around various places in your area, telling them about the history and other aspects of what they are seeing. In general, the area will be defined by geographical boundaries, and your level of knowledge about this area must be high and very detailed.

In addition to such tours, you might develop a speciality, such as tours of gardens, industrial archaeology, or the music of a certain period, and these may take you further afield.

Most guides will accompany tourists in whatever transport is provided for them, but some take small groups in their own cars or mini-buses; these are known as 'driver' guides.

*Further Information:* The following organisation can provide more information about becoming a tourist guide, and in particular about the 'Blue Badge' qualification which guides need in order to gain access to the best-paying work

The Guild of Registered Tourist Guides (and the Association of Driver Guides)
Guild House
52d Borough High Street
London
SE1 1XN
Tel: 020 7403 1115
Web: www.blue-badge-guides.com

## 44. Toy Making

As with all hand-made products, making toys puts you in competition with the cheap plastic items coming in from the Far East and other low-wage economies. You will therefore need to aim your toys at fond parents who are prepared to pay extra for good quality. Such parents are often of the 'green' persuasion, and will look more kindly on toys made from natural materials (such as wood) from sustainable resources. They also like educational toys and those of traditional patterns, such as chickens on a board which peck when you pull a string, rocking horses or Noah's Arks. Here you have to find the right balance between toys which will appeal to children and those which their parents (who pay for them) think appropriate. Another possibility is making specialised items for the enthusiasts who collect such things as teddy bears, doll's houses or antique-style dolls.

*Further Information:* Part-time courses in toy making are run at many local colleges and adult education centres. One institution that regularly offers such courses is South Thames College.

South Thames College
Wandsworth High Street
Wandsworth
London
SW18 2PP
Tel. 020 8918 7777
Web: www.south-thames.ac.uk

## 45. Translation

If you have a good knowledge of a foreign language, offering a translation service could be the ideal home-based business for you. Much translation work is technical or commercial, so in addition to your language skills it will help if you have some specialist knowledge of a particular topic: computers, medicine or the law, for example. Highly technical translations are generally the best paid (and most difficult). The more obscure languages command the highest rates of pay, though the demand for such translations is likely to be less frequent than for 'mainstream' languages such as French and German.

Translation work tends to be irregular, and many freelance translators combine it with other work such as language teaching and interpreting.

*Further Information:* The Institute of Translation and Interpreting (ITI) is a professional organisation aiming to promote high standards in translating and interpreting. Membership is open to anyone with a 'genuine and proven' interest in translating and interpreting. Members receive a range of services, including information (and discounts) on courses and conferences, and a bi-monthly bulletin. The ITI also offers a free referral service, whereby enquirers can be given the names of suitable members for any translating or interpreting assignment.

Institute of Translation and Interpreting
Fortuna House
South Fifth Street
Milton Keynes
MK9 2EU
Tel: 01908 325250
Web: www.iti.org.uk

## 46. Typing and Word Processing

If you have good typing skills you could put these to use running your own home-based typing and/or word processing business. There is still a need for basic copy- and audio-typing services, but increasingly nowadays clients are likely to expect word processing as well. To offer a word processing (not just typing) service, you will of course need a modern computer word processor. This will allow you to perform many additional tasks not possible – or possible only with difficulty – on an ordinary typewriter, e.g. saving documents in electronic form, to be stored, updated and printed again later as required.

You may find your services easier to sell if you offer a range of additional secretarial and clerical services, for example, telephone answering, filing, envelope-stuffing, and so on.

*Further Information:* If you need to polish your typing or word processing skills, most colleges and adult education centres offer a range of part-time courses. Your local library should be able to give you more information.

## 47. Video Production

Modern camcorders are lightweight, inexpensive and – used with a modicum of skill and judgment – can produce highly professional-looking results. This has presented an ideal opportunity for home-based businessmen and women to turn an interest in this form of photography into a paying business.

The range of potential markets for video photographers (or videographers, as they are sometimes called) is vast. Wedding videos are probably the single largest source of work. However, there is a huge range of other events for which a video may also be required, including speeches, concerts, dance and theatrical productions, parties, sporting events and award presentations. Some estate agents engage videographers to produce videos of houses to show to prospective purchasers; while up-and-coming pop groups and bands may require a videographer's services to produce a 'promo' for them.

*Further Information:* A leading organisation in this field is the Guild of Professional Videographers. Guild members receive a range of benefits, including meetings, a monthly newsletter, and the opportunity to buy equipment at trade prices. The Guild also refers enquiries from potential clients to suitably qualified members.

The Guild of Professional Videographers
11 Telfer Road
Radford
Coventry
West Midlands
CV6 3DG
Tel: 024 7627 2548
Web: www.gpv4u.co.uk

## 48. Website Design

Website designers combine technical, writing and design skills to produce attractive-looking web pages which show off their clients to good effect and help them sell more of their products and services. They advise clients on the best way to promote themselves via the Internet, and show them examples of what can be done. Clients generally provide at least a rough draft of the text they want on their site and any artwork or photographs. Website designers then create the sites on their computer, using programs specially designed for this purpose. Once clients are satisfied with their sites, the designer makes the necessary arrangements to publish them on the World Wide Web.

As well as creating and publishing sites, website designers also often assist clients in promoting them, e.g. by ensuring that they are listed on all the leading Internet search engines. Finally, they may retain responsibility for revising and updating sites (for which they receive an additional fee).

*Further Information:* Courses in website design are widely available at local colleges and adult education centres. There are also several good introductory books on the subject, e.g. 'Web Design: A Complete Introduction' by Dr Nigel Chapman and Jenny Chapman (Wiley). As you might expect, there are also plenty of websites offering advice and information in this field. One good instructional site for both beginners and those who already have some knowledge of HTML (the main language in which websites are written) is Page Tutor at www.pagetutor.com.

A range of home-study courses in website design is offered by the Distance Learning Centre.

The Distance Learning Centre
Swaledale
4 Coaley Lane
Newbottle
Houghton le Spring
Tyne & Wear
DH4 4SQ
Tel: 0845 129 7238
Web: www.distance-learning-centre.co.uk

## 49. Will Writing

Will writing, rather like conveyancing, is one of those legal tasks which do not have to be carried out by a qualified solicitor, and which has developed into a separate profession. Many will writers also offer a service which helps lay executors obtain grants of probate, and some (by no means all) are also prepared to serve as executors themselves.

*Further Information:* The Institute of Professional Will Writers offers advice and assistance to members and prospective members. It offers a one-day introductory course to people who are thinking of taking up will-writing and want to know more about it. They then offer a three-day intensive course, leading up to a professional examination.

The Institute of Professional Will Writers
Trinity Point
New Road
Halesowen
West Midlands
B63 3HY
Tel: 08456 442042
Web: www.ipw.org.uk

## 50. Window Cleaning

If you enjoy working in the open air and have a reasonable head for heights, window cleaning could be the business for you. The actual requirements to get started in this field are minimal. And one big advantage of the window cleaning business is that, once you have built up a round, your customers will want you back every three weeks or so to repeat the job.

One possible drawback of window cleaning is that it is somewhat seasonal. It is impossible to work in very bad weather, and clients will generally not expect to see you in the depths of winter. Because of this, many window cleaners have another source of income to help see them through the darker months, e.g. interior decorating or 'odd-jobbing'.

*Further Information:* The National Federation of Master Window and General Cleaners can provide advice and information on all aspects of window cleaning. They also stock a range of professional window cleaning equipment, available to members at trade prices.

National Federation of Master Window and General Cleaners
Summerfield House
Harrogate Road
Reddish
Stockport
Cheshire
SK5 6HH
Tel: 0161 432 8754
Web: www.nfmwgc.com

## 51. Writing

Writing is one of the most popular home-based business opportunities. The range of potential outlets for freelance writers is vast, including magazines and newspaper articles, short stories, non-fiction books, novels, TV and radio, filmscripts, plays, advertising copywriting, poetry, greetings card slogans, and more.

Writing is, however, a highly competitive field, and it can take time – perhaps several years – to build enough business to generate a respectable full-time income. Many people start part-time, perhaps writing articles or short stories in the evenings and weekends, and this method has much to recommend it.

*Further Information:* One popular approach is to take a distance-learning course. The UK's leading provider of such courses is The Writers Bureau. They offer a comprehensive course in creative writing, as well as more specialised courses in specific areas such as short story writing and writing for children.

The Writers Bureau
Sevendale House
7 Dale Street
Manchester
M1 1JB
Tel: 0161 228 2362
Web: www.writersbureau.com

If you wish to become a freelance journalist, it is well worth joining the National Union of Journalists (NUJ), who have an active freelance branch.

National Union of Journalists
Acorn House
308-312 Gray's Inn Road
London
WC1X 8DP
Tel: 020 7278 7916
Web: www.nuj.org.uk and www.londonfreelance.org (the website of the NUJ freelance branch)

# appendix

## Useful Organisations

The Advertising Standards Authority
Mid City Place
71 High Holborn
London
WC1V 6QT
Tel: 020 7492 2222
Web: www.asa.org.uk

Asset Based Finance Association
(formerly Factors and Discounters
Association)
Boston House
The Little Green
Richmond
Surrey
TW9 1QE
Tel: 020 8332 9955
Web: www.abfa.org.uk

Association of British Insurers
51 Gresham Street
London
EC2V 7HQ
Tel: 020 7600 3333
Web: www.abi.org.uk

British Agents Register
5A Cheltenham Mount
Harrogate
North Yorkshire
HG1 1DW
Tel: 01423 560608
Web: www.agentsregister.co.uk

British Chambers of Commerce
4 Westwood House
Westwood Business Park
Coventry
CV4 8HS
Tel: 024 7669 4484
Web: www.britishchambers.org.uk

British Franchise Association
Thames View
Newtown Road
Henley-on-Thames
Oxon
RG9 1HG
Tel: 01491 578050
Web: www.thebfa.org

British Standards Institution
389 Chiswick High Road
London
W4 4AL
Tel: 020 8996 9001
Web: www.bsi-global.com

Business in the Community (BITC)
137 Shepherdess Walk
London
N1 7RQ
Tel: 020 7566 8650
Web: www.bitc.org.uk

Chartered Institute of Patent Attorneys
95 Chancery Lane
London
WC2A 1DT
Tel: 020 7405 9450
Web: www.cipa.org.uk

Chartered Management Institute
(formerly Institute of Management)
Management House
Cottingham Road
Corby
Northants
NN17 1TT
Tel: 01536 204222
Web: www.managers.org.uk

Crafts Council
44a Pentonville Road
London
N1 9BY
Tel: 020 7278 7700
Web: www.craftscouncil.org.uk

Department for Business, Enterprise and
Regulatory Reform
1 Victoria Street
London
SW1H 0ET
Tel: 020 7215 5000
Web: www.dti.gov.uk

Direct Mail Information Service
Mail Media Centre
Stukely Street
London
WC1V 7AB
Tel: 020 7421 2250
Web: www.dmis.co.uk

Direct Marketing Association
DMA House
70 Margaret Street
London
W1W 8SS
Tel: 020 7291 3300
Web: www.dma.org.uk

Direct Selling Association
29 Floral Street
London
WC2 9DP
Tel: 020 7497 1234
Web: www.dsa.org.uk

Enterprise Nation
Redbrick Enterprises Ltd
Redbrick House
9 Town Walls
Shrewsbury
Shropshire
SY1 1TW
Tel: 01743 272555
Web: www.enterprisenation.com
Organisation for home-based business
owners

Federation of Small Businesses
Whittle Way
Blackpool Business Park
Blackpool
Lancashire
FY4 2FE
Tel: 01253 336000
Web: www.fsb.org.uk

Finance and Leasing Association
2nd Floor, Imperial House
15-19 Kingsway
London
WC2B 6UN
Tel: 020 7836 6511
Web: www.fla.org.uk

Financial Ombudsman Service
South Quay Plaza
183 Marsh Wall
London E14 9SR
Tel: 020 7964 1000
Web: www.financial-ombudsman.org.uk

Forum of Private Business
Ruskin Chambers
Drury Lane
Knutsford
Cheshire
WA16 6HA
Tel: 01565 634467
Web: www.fpb.org

Highlands and Islands Enterprise
Cowan House
Inverness Retail and Business Park
Inverness
IV2 7GF
Tel: 01463 234171
Web: www.hie.co.uk

Home Business Alliance
Werrington Business Centre
86 Papyrus Road
Peterborough
PE4 5BH
Tel: 0871 474 1015
Web: www.homebusiness.org.uk

Information Commissioner's Office
(formerly Data Protection Registrar)
Wycliffe House
Water Lane
Wilmslow
Cheshire
SK9 5AF
Tel: 08456 30 60 60
Web: www.ico.gov.uk

Institute of Directors
116 Pall Mall
London
SW1Y 5ED
Tel: 020 7839 1233
Web: www.iod.co.uk

Market Research Society
15 Northburgh Street
London
EC1V 0AH
Tel: 020 7490 4911
Web: www.mrs.org.uk

National Federation of Enterprise Agencies
12 Stephenson Court
Fraser Road
Priory Business Park
Bedford
MK44 3WJ
Tel: 01234 831623
Web: www.nfea.com

Office of Fair Trading
Fleetbank House
2-6 Salisbury Square
London
EC4Y 8JX
Tel: 020 7211 8000
Web: www.oft.gov.uk

The Prince's Trust
18 Park Square East
London
NW1 4LH
Tel: 020 7543 1234
Web: www.princes-trust.org

Registrar of Companies
Companies Registration Office
Crown Way
Maindy
Cardiff
CF4 3UZ
Tel: 0870 33 33 636
Web: www.companieshouse.co.uk

Scottish Enterprise
FREEPOST SCO7559
Glasgow
G2 8BR
Tel: 0845 607 8787
Web: www.scottish-enterprise.com

Shell LiveWIRE Programme
Design Works Unit 15
William Street
Felling
Gateshead
Tyne & Wear
NE10 0JP
Tel: 0845 757 3252
Web: www.shell-livewire.org

The Telework Association
No contact address given
Tel: 0800 616008
Web: www.telework.org.uk
Organisation for home-based workers

UK Intellectual Property Office
(formerly the Patent Office)
Concept House
Cardiff Road
Newport
South Wales
NP10 8QQ
Tel: 01633 813930
Web: www.ipo.gov.uk

UK Trade & Investment Service
(formerly British Trade International)
Tay House
300 Bath Street
Glasgow
G2 4DX
Tel: 020 7215 8000
Web: www.uktradeinvest.gov.uk